The Salt Maker of Maldon

GILLIAN SOUDAH

Ian Henry Publications

The cover: Cyril Osborne stoking one of the furnaces

British Library Cataloguing in Publication Data

Soudah, Gillian
  The salt maker of Maldon.
  1. Osborne, Cyril   2. Salt industry and
  trade —— England —— Maldon (Essex) ——
  Biography
  I. Title
  622'.363'0924   HD9213.G7208

  ISBN 0-86025-414-3

Printed by **Booksprint**
1a Marsh Lane, Ashton, Bristol BS3 2NR
for
Ian Henry Publications, Ltd.,
20 Park Drive, Romford, Essex RM1 4LH

INTRODUCTION

As a tribute to my father I have written his biography, for I know he would have been pleased for his memories and experiences to be put into print – they are now a part of history, bygones, never to return, only seen in the imagination through his words.

He was born in the era when it was believed that little children should be seen and not heard, when horses were the main source of transport and when street corner entertainment with dancing bears and monkeys performing to the sounds of barrel organ music was appreciated.

Interested and observant, he was always able to recall, with feeling, the colourful events that took place at the Rose & Crown, where he was born. His apprenticeship days as an electrical engineer were often hazardous, as well as unusual, compared to those of today.

Finally in 1932 he entered the family business of the Maldon Crystal Salt Company to become a salt maker, carrying on the traditions of the area. Without modern aids it was no easy task – coal carting, stoking furnaces, handling tons of salt each day. It wasn't until the more prosperous days of the 70s when modernisation made the salt maker's life easier.

The key to the mould into which Father fitted has been lost forever, for he has taken it with him and, as they say, "They don't make them like that any more".

Cyril Osborne

THE EARLY YEARS

On 26th March, 1985, the Union Jack flew at half mast, the Salt Works were silent, the furnaces switched off and the packing room empty, no salt would be made that day. These were the marks of respect for my Father whose life had ended that day and whose involvement in the Works had lasted most of his seventy-seven years.

All that day I could hear his voice in my mind repeating the tales he had told me: so many interesting and unusual events that he never tired of relating to me and I never tired of hearing. Right back to his childhood days he could remember, through his youth and later, enabling me to imagine the atmosphere of an age I never knew. He was a natural story teller with the gift of humour, not studied or practiced, it all flowed without effort. I had felt many times that I would like to write his story, never doing any- thing about it; now I knew the time had come for me to record his colourful life.

"I remember," he would begin, as he recalled events, bringing the past to life. Details, names and happenings were recollected with clarity, to be vouched for by friends and relatives who were also there. "Marvellous," he would say, "I can remember things like that, yet if you asked me who I met last week I'd have a job to recall that."

Most of the people who knew him will associate my Father with the Maldon Salt Works. I shall tell also of his life leading up to that association; I am remembering him remembering.

In 1907 Nellie and Edward Osborne were the proprietors of the White Lion public house at the foot of Market Hill, Maldon. It is no longer a pub and has changed its identity to Ferns Restaurant, but anyone interested can still see the evidence that it was once an inn. Father pointed this out to me for, as you look up on the outside wall of the restaurant, you can still discern the faded words 'Good Stabling'. Visitors could rest their horses, while themselves sleeping in the White Lion. Travelling entertainers, with their performing bears and monkeys, could stay there and use the cellars for the animals to rest. The morning would see them led away on chains to perform to the music of barrel organs – an accepted entertainment of the times.

That December Nellie and Edward, with their two young sons, moved to a larger and busier licensed house in the High Street, the Rose & Crown. Less than a month later Nellie bore a third son, Cyril Bernard, my Father. He was the son who brought most joy to his Mother during her hard working life.

Cyril was about three years old when he first became aware of the busy life surrounding him. The hubbub of the popular bar, clinking of glasses, ringing of the till, loud voices drifting through the smoky atmosphere, together with the odour of overworked sweaty bodies and the slamming of doors as people came and went. There was also the occasional noise of a slot machine, a bird singing and a tune from the pianola, but money was scarce and mostly spent on another pint, rather than games or tunes.

A bar known as the slipway was a small, ill-lit space, used by customers who appeared anxious not to be seen, like the unkempt woman, her age difficult to judge in the half light, who took her drink quickly and disappeared, or there were those bringing their jugs to be filled with ale.

In winter a large coal fire welcomed customers in the public bar, but not everyone was able to take advantage of the warmth, for a greedy few crowded around the fire warming their backsides. Edward, concerned that not all his customers were benefitting from the fire, had a large notice displayed over the mantlepiece, "Please do not stand before this fire, Pray sit down is my desire, So other folk as well as you, May see this fire and feel it too. Thank you." That seemed to do the trick.

Nellie Osborne had very little time to share with her boys and many motherly duties were carried out by the maids, who put them to bed with the occasional bedtime story. Cyril often used to be frightened as he lay in bed at night, listening to a gruff voice rumbling in the slip bar beneath his bedroom floor. He would cover his ears trying to blot out a voice so terrifying to a small boy. Old Jim Bush would have been most upset had he known, for he had a gentle character not in keeping with his voice.

A public house was a demanding occupation; besides serving drinks over the counter, there was the added responsibility of preparing and cooking food for cycling and char-a-banc parties. Maldon was a popular resort.

While Nellie ran the Rose & Crown, her husband added to their income with an extra business based in their yard. He was a haulier and, in those days, that meant horse and cart. Renowned as a strong man, in fact, the strongest in the town, although his physique did not suggest this, he could lift things beyond the capacities of most men. That must have been a great asset to him, when his loads could consist of such items as sacks of corn, furniture, even tombstones. Anything moveable could be collected and delivered in his cart within Maldon and the Dengie Hundred.

After just such a day in 1911 he returned home unusually tired and complained of feeling unwell.

"It's probably a chill," Nellie suggested. "You'd better go up to bed, I'll bring you some hot soup."

Keeping her word, she later carried the soup on a tray to his room, but Edward lay motionless in bed; life had deserted him in his late thirties. The doctor's verdict was a strained heart and no wonder, thinking of his heavy work.

His wife was stunned from the shock, remaining in her room for several days, refusing to eat and without sleep. Friends and relatives were alarmed for her mental and physical health, but they need not have worried, she was a fighter and had no intention of giving up. Gathering her resources, she engaged a charlady to clean and extra staff to help with bar duties and continued to run the Rose & Crown, as well as bring up her three sons.

As Cyril was only 3 at the time he was shielded as much as possible from the sorrow of losing his father. He recalled little of his death or, indeed, much about him at all, except for being carried shoulder high to bed at night.

Recently I met a lady who actually recalled attending the funeral with her parents. She was only 6 at the time. Her white spotted muslin dress had been carefully threaded with black ribbon for the occasion, while others attending the funeral wore black armbands. The funeral was held on a Sunday for that was the only day that would not disrupt the running of business at the Rose & Crown. As the horse-drawn coffin started on its journey to the church curtains were drawn along the route, people sighting the procession stopped, the men removing their caps, signs of respect in a less busy age.

As time passed it was noticed that an eligible bachelor, an athlete and champion cyclist with many medals and trophies to his credit, was to be seen at the Rose & Crown. Jim Rivers, in his late twenties, courted and married Nellie Osborne, ten years his senior.

Now there was another business to run as the Rivers family owned the Queen Street Dairies, where now stands Triad Electricals. Their cattle and horses were kept on the Longfields across the road. Jim Rivers also had a mill where he operated as a miniature hasler, dealing in chaff, straw, hay, wheat, oats, mangels and turnips. Inside the mill was an old diesel engine generating the power needed to crush and chop the animal feeds that he sold to help maintain the dairy business. Now, shrub and grassland cover the spot where the old mill stood, near the entrance to the

Wantz Road Nurseries.

My father claimed "Pop had the flashiest milk float in the town". The three boys had given their step-father that affectionate title, with which he seemed well pleased and they called him 'Pop' until the end.

"I can see the milk float now, drawn by one of the best hackneys in Maldon. The big shining brass milk churn stood in the centre of the float, on the side of which was the brass name plate 'J Rivers, Queen Street Dairies'. Pop would ring a small brass bell attached to the side of the float to announce his arrival at the customer's house. The horse became so familiar with the regular daily round that he stopped automatically outside customers' houses. Jim would take his smaller can full of milk and measure out the customers' requirements into their jugs left standing on the doorsteps. Sometimes they only wanted as little as a quarter of a pint. They left the book with the milk jug and the amount was entered so they could pay up at the end of the week."

Cyril often recalled this scene with the hackney stepping out smartly, pulling the milk float with the bright polished brass churn in the middle. It must have made quite an impression on him as a small boy, feeling proud that he was part of it all.

Nellie blessed her good fortune in her marriage to a younger man willing to take on a ready made family. So it could have been understandable that she may have kept an unnecessarily jealous eye on attractive housemaids. Any suspicion that her husband's thoughts might be roving in that direction would cause her to dismiss that maid: better to be safe than sorry! It seemed that all was well and Jim never broke his marriage vows.

He and his stepsons had one thing, above all, in common – the drive to make money. They never shirked work and would keep going all the hours that God made. From an early age my Father helped his parents, they needed every available hand. The day started at 6 a.m. at the Rose & Crown. The maids would first rake and clean out the

5

smouldering embers from the coal grates and stove. At times, re-lighting the fires could prove to be a difficult operation when the wood was damp. The big cast-iron stove just outside the kitchen door would roar away belching black smoke from the metal chimney just above the stove. The water for the bathroom would soon be hot and appreciated by the guests, as before they had had water carried to their rooms in a jug to be used in the china basin on the wash-stand.

The bar floor was stone slabs then, stark as a monastery and needing to be scrubbed every day after the customers' boots had trodden them. Spittoons had to be emptied each day, not a pleasant job, and filled again with fresh sawdust. Spittoons would be frowned upon today, but in those days of tobacco chewing, the 'old boys' who came to the pub needed somewhere to spit. Even if they didn't chew, the spittoons were still used. The 'fags' the poorer men smoked were rough and strong, sometimes rolled from loose tobacco: sometimes they searched the street gutters for 'dog ends' and puffed away at the remains. It wasn't surprising that many died long before reaching three score years and ten.

The ceilings of the Rose & Crown were yellow as mustard, due to the customers' smoking. The atmosphere was so thick on a busy Saturday night that the smoke could be re-directed with a sharp movement of the hand. Small wonder that Nellie suffered from bad bouts of bronchitis in the winter, although she wasn't a smoker - but might as well have been, as she inhaled large daily doses of her customers' output.

Another thing that Father recalled from those early days of horse power was the manger in the yard, filled with chaff and corn, so that when a carrier or merchant wanted a pint, he would put a measure of this feed into the horse's nose-bag to be strapped under the nose, so the animal could feed contentedly while its driver had a drink. If he was away too long the horse might finish its feed and become impatient, scraping its hooves on the cobbled stone floor, making a noise that could be heard in the bar. Then it was time to move on – or re-fill the bag.

The yard was often noisy with the sound of horses' hooves, for here many sales took place. The wheeling and dealing was generally swift, for the two parties concerned slapped their hands together uttering the word 'done', this one word signifying an agreement of sale had been reached.

At that time horses were as essential to business as motor transport is today. To carry out the duties required of them the horses had to be strong and sound in wind and limb. Pop with his expert eye for a horse would take his time in choosing his purchase; first he would run his hand up and down the horse's legs feeling for any imperfections: he would detect any scars on the knees however well they may have been disguised, for a horse with such knees would be less valuable, as it could never be trusted not to fall again. He would run the horse up and down the yard testing for any signs of lameness and, at the same time, listen to its breathing for fear it was broken winded.

Father would say, "Pop knew his onions where horses were concerned".

The Rose & Crown

THE OUTING

Heavy black clouds and rumbling thunder preceeded the large spots of rain that splashed down on the newly erected marquee in the yard of the Rose & Crown. Soon rivulets of water began to seep through wherever there was a small crack in the canvas dampening some of the seats and staining the crisply laundered tablecloths covering yards of trestle tables.

This set the scene for an outing of two hundred people. Cyril had taken part in the furious activity of the previous day preparing for this event. Cohen Weenen & Co., Ltd., large cigarette manufacturers of the day, were giving a staff outing and had chosen the Rose & Crown at Maldon. Many people were familiar with this firm and their outings. Undaunted by the weather, which later cleared, turning to sun and blue skies, everyone went full steam ahead for the great day; wet cloths were changed on the tables and chairs dried.

A field kitchen had been set up in a corner of the yard to cope with cooking the large amounts of food that would be consumed when the visitors sat down. Huge joints of succulent beef stood on the kitchen table awaiting Pop, who would carve with his razor-sharp knife to fill the plates with meat. Nellie worked furiously in the hot kitchen – and her glasses slipped straight into the bowl of Yorkshire pudding mix. Father didn't say what happened then, but presumably the spectacles were rescued and the pudding was none the worse.

Walls and ceiling dripped with condensation, the only air coming in was from a small window facing a brick wall. Perhaps it was just as well that not too much air blew from the direction of the wall that hid the men's toilets from view of the window and also the open gully, down which flowed the end result of a few pints of beer.

The first char-a-banc arrived as the rain cleared completely and the passengers, as they came into the yard, were a happy noisy crowd that had alighted from the ten coaches stretching bonnet to tail down the High Street. Each vehicle carried between twenty and twenty-five people, so the crowd can be imagined. They beseiged the bar and freshly pulled pints frothing over pewter mugs filled the counter top, together with soft drinks and spirits.

On the stroke of 2 o'clock, after doing a roaring trade, Pop called, "Time, gentlemen, please!" Eventually the visitors were persuaded from the bars and into the marquee for lunch.

It was in a very merry and festive mood they all sat down at the long tables laden with roast beef, Yorkshire pudding and dishes of vegetables, served by lady helpers, engaged for the occasion, arrayed in frilly white aprons and caps.

Father talked a great deal about these events – for an outing was an event 70 years ago, when it was not the norm for every family to have a car and the only way to get about was by horse, train or char-a-banc. As people also had fewer and shorter holidays they packed their enjoyment into such outings. Cyril was absorbed into the atmosphere of jollity and was thoroughly impressed by it all: he even remembered the names of the people who worked at these lunches, mentioning Mrs Scarriot as a valuable helper.

When the coaches at last pulled away, there were still the regular customers to serve and work to be done before everyone could go to bed. There were glasses to be washed, barrels to be changed and bottles to be brought up from the cellar. There may have been food orders at suppertime, anything from cold meat and pickles to deep fried fish.

On occasions, when justice was not done to all the food cooked, the left-overs, such as joints of meat, were given to the helpers to take home to their families to eat, for there were no 'fridges or freezers in general use and the only means of keeping food for even a short time was to store it in the cellar, where the temperature was cool on the hottest of days or in a meat safe – a cupboard made of wire mesh, keeping the meat from the flies that buzzed frustratedly around it in a useless effort to get inside.

When Cyril, who was brought up in the school of 'little boys must be seen and not heard', was older he helped prepare the vegetables, peeling potatoes and shelling peas until his fingers were sore. Having been given permission from his mother, he set up a 'wash and brush up' in the yard, charging tuppence a time. Whenever a party visited the Rose & Crown this amenity was available and Father admitted, years later, that some of the proceeds from this service had gone towards buying his first motorbike. He made the stand out of orange boxes that carried a bowl of water, some soap and a towel. There was also a mirror for those concerned about their appearance. As customers left by the gate they might be tempted to spend more of their coppers on a bunch of flowers, which had been picked from Old Man Tunmer's garden nearby and were on sale at sixpence a bunch – or whatever the customer would offer, which was probably a lot less. Collecting and selling jam jars was another of Cyril's occasional occupations to get him a few more pennies to spend, but more often than not he saved his money.

One day there was an outing of employees from West Ham Borough Council. They were a particularly rough crowd, who had started drinking on the journey. If Sergeant Spurling of the local police had had any idea they were coming he would not have cared that they had a booking in the town: he didn't want their trouble. So strict was he that it was said if he caught anyone bending down tying their shoelace, he would have them for obstruction.

However, the party arrived at the Rose & Crown; when they entered the marquee they found the top executive table was set with wine, but not theirs, so they raided it. A fight started, stopping just short of a riot. The food went back to the kitchen, for the party was in no fit state to eat it. They were the losers as they had paid in advance.

On another occasion the piano in the bar was being played much louder than usual, accompanied by strange voices. Cyril was curious, but afraid of discovery, he crept down the passage leading to the bar pressed against the wall and looked in. He couldn't hear what was being said, but suddenly someone slammed the piano lid on to the player's fingers. Fighting started amongst the strangers, mugs and glasses flying. One man was about to be lynched by the mob and, before the boy's astonished eyes, his mother leaned over the bar counter and dragged the man to safety on her side. The police were called, but never came – "Too bloody frightened", was the general opinion.

Pop's interest in cycling prompted him to welcome the parties of cyclists who converged on the Rose & Crown at Bank Holidays, when about twenty at a time would be accommodated for bed and breakfast, sometimes six in a bed, but all strictly above board – no mixed doubles! Males slept in separate quarters well apart from the girls, Nellie made sure of that.

Then, as the summer season faded out, work did not, for the Rose & Crown catered for all the dances held at the Parish Hall, as well as for weddings and funerals. Big or small, all parties were welcomed.

There were some colourful personalities in the town then. One of the most noticeable, by his size and by his occupation was 'Sipper' Norton. A giant of a man, standing six foot, six inches, with a girth three times that of an average man, he was the Town Crier. He stood in the High Street, outside the Moot Hall, ringing his large brass bell and shouting in his deep, loud voice, "Oh, yea. Oh, yea," as a prelude to any announcement he had to make in order to be heard above the street noises.

Sipper Norton was a regular at the Rose & Crown and was reputed to have an unquenchable thirst. Pop would pull a pint for him, in his old embossed pewter mug, but before he could put Sipper's money in the till, the pint would have gone: he would open his mouth, tip the mug and down slipped the beer.

"Fill it up, Jim, that's only a wet," two or three more pints of beer would disappear in as many minutes and Sipper would leave the bar just as quickly.

Another character my Father recalled was Hardy King. He and Frank Wilding used to drink together in the King's Head and make fantastic bets with each other. Frank was the Chief Marshal of Ceremonies, which meant that he would walk in front of the horse drawn hearse at official funerals. The hearse could be best described as a glass box on wheels with the coffin inside in full view. Straw was laid along the street, so that the funeral could proceed along the street with quiet and dignity. After he had been on duty he would appear at the pub, still dressed in his long black frock coat and silk tophat, ready for one of his bets.

The two men had taken a goose to the pub and Wilding made a bet with Hardy King that he would get his goose to drink beer. When it wouldn't oblige voluntarily they poured ale down its throat and the poor thing ended up rolling on the floor in a drunken state. Who won the bet is uncertain.

There was always the odd poacher who frequented the bar dressed in a tattered cumbersome coat with a secret inside pocket where he carried his 'loot', often a brace of rabbits, sometimes a pheasant or a partridge. "How much yer give us for 'em, Guv?" he would say holding out his poached game for inspection. "Must be worth a pint or two," Pop would say. The poacher was usually grateful for anything offered and would either stay and drink the proceeds or slip the money into his pocket and leave.

There was a recluse living in a derelict hut at Beeleigh. People were naturally curious about such a person, who they called Dumpling Dick. The venturesome young lads who explored the area took delight in terrifying themselves by creeping as close to his hut as possible and then jeering at him. At the very sight of this scarecrow figure waving his arms to give chase, sent the boys into a frenzy, when they ran for their lives, although he was known to be harmless. The authorities tried to persuade Dick to leave the hut for somewhere more comfortable many times, but Dick defended his territory aggressively, staying in his residence until his death.

Cyril Bernard Osborne in 1909

CHILDHOOD MEMORIES

One of Father's most vivid memories during his early child-hood days was when Pop met with an almost fatal accident in the summer of 1912.

He had been working at the time in his mill near Long-fields, where the old diesel engine had chugged away noisily for hours providing the power to chop and crush the chaff and oats, some of which had already been bagged, while the rest lay in a heap to be dealt with the following day.

Daylight had started to fade as Pop took a handsome hunter attached to a silver chain from his waistcoat pocket and was surprised to find that time had slipped away so quickly, already making him late for his evening meal. As he switched off the old diesel engine and turned to leave, the flap of his jacket caught in the key way of the still—revolving fly wheel. Like a giant hand it plucked him off the ground and whirled him round and round before finally stopping, but not before his legs had been crushed and bent backwards. His cries for help were eventually heard by two passing workmen, who were shocked at his injuries and the lacerations to his face and chest. "He looks nearly a gonna to me," whispered one of the men, as Pop, deathly white, moaned through painful spasms of breathing.

There was a sheep's hurdle lying in the corner of the barn and, after covering it with a thick layer of straw, they used it as a stretcher to carry him home. Nellie, having collected her thoughts after the initial shock of seeing Pop lying on the hurdle, asked the men to carry him upstairs to the bedroom, which wasn't an easy operation as the staircase was steep and narrow with an awkward bend.

The doctor who had been summoned to the Rose & Crown took time in examining his patient and found to his dismay that the injuries were such that he did not have the means to cure them. Nellie was waiting outside the bedroom door when the doctor emerged and knew instantly, from the look on his face before he spoke, that there was little hope of Pop's recovery. The doctor's firm grip on her arm guided her along the landing to the stairway, where he stopped and faced her. Reluctantly he told her, "Mrs Rivers, I have to tell you there is nothing else that can be done for your husband and I think you should know I don't expect him to last the night."

She did not answer for fear of breaking down, but returned to the bedroom where she sat and held his hand, there being nothing else she could do. He was still conscious, but Nellie wished he would pass out for a while, she could see his pain was so great – there were no pain killers in those days, a person just had to put up with it. She sat with him during what she thought were his last hours and the night wore on. Exhausted, she fell asleep until dawn broke and rain, splashing against the window, woke her.

Pop groaned and then asked for a glass of water. He had lived through the night and the crisis was over for now. He could not be moved to the hospital at Chelmsford, ten miles away, as he was too ill. He needed to be X-rayed, but that was impossible and it was only by feel that the doctor found he also had broken ribs. An almost severed finger was stitched back into place. There was a kind of incubator treatment for his damaged legs to help prevent the tendons shrinking.

His recovery was slow and he was never to be as fit again, for he always walked with a slight limp and experienced bouts of pain. The shock of the accident brought on attacks of asthma, from which he suffered for the rest of his life, but his enthusiasm for work was not destroyed. These disabilities – and a permanently bent finger – were constant reminders of his near fatal accident. Pop maintained that the sovereign case he carried in his top pocket saved his life. It was positioned in such a way that the machinery flattened the case, damaging the coins inside, but preventing further injury to his chest.

The year following was difficult, for all that time Pop was recovering from his accident. His aging parents continued to run the Queen Street Dairies as best they could after having reduced the number of cattle grazing Longfields, for Pop was unable to channel as much energy into the business as before. Eventually the inevitable decision had to be taken to sell the business, together with the many acres of grazing land.

Pop, never one to rest for long, was already hatching the idea of a car for hire business, which came into being some years later.

In the meantime, the Rose & Crown carried on with the many activities associated with inn life, including the running of a goose club in common with most other pubs. Through the year 'regulars' would pay in a small sum of sixpence or a shilling weekly, although some may have paid more. This meant they had something put by for Christmas, as well as the added enjoyment of 'paying out night' when it was usual for the landlord to give a free drink to every 'investor'.

"Why are they called goose clubs?" Cyril asked his mother. Her logical answer was that it may have been because the first prize in the club draw was a goose. There were also chickens, ducks and rabbits as other prizes. Before the advent of the American turkey, a goose was the traditional British Christmas dinner.

Trade would be slow as the winter started: it wasn't until the clubs paid out a week before Christmas that there were any visible signs that the Festive Season was so close. The church choirs and other organised – or disorganised

– bands of carol singers would then start to sing on town doorsteps, not daring to knock before singing through a repertoire of carols; householders wanted their entertainment before they paid, even if it was only a penny or two. Sometimes the reward was just a few mincepies. The church choirs gave the best performances, as they stood and sang the favourite carols tunefully, gathered round their lantern attached to a long pole.

On his way to school the boy would search the shop windows as he passed for signs of Christmas coming. When he saw they were clearing the display and putting up paper chains, glittering tinsel and coloured glass baubles, his heart raced in excitement, for it meant the great day was very near.

On Christmas Eve Cyril lay fidgetting in bed, tired but unable to sleep, fixing his eyes on the two empty knee socks hanging at the bottom of the bed. He started to get worried for he still believed, as do so many little boys, that Santa would not come down the chimney with his presents until he was asleep. Getting down the chimney would be no problem as the fireplace in his room was large enough to stand in and gaze up the lofty chimney stack to see the glow of the moon and twinkling stars in the frosty night sky. He dropped off eventually, to awake in the morning to find the socks filled with sweets, nuts and an orange. A white string stocking was also at the foot of the bed filled with trivialities, such as a pair of tin scales, balloons, a whistle and more sweetmeats.

After the joy of the Christmas stocking the best was yet to come. Downstairs his parents waited to give him a train set; this special present from them was always the biggest delight of Christmas for my father. He never forgot one Christmas when his brother, Cliff, played a cruel trick on him. While Cyril slept Cliff took away his socks filled with presents, replacing them with ashes.

Being of a sensitive nature he was often saddened when the time came for the maids to receive their presents, for the Christmas wrappers usually only contained a frilly

17

white apron or cap and he felt their unexpressed hopes, for this was probably the only gift they received.

Life continued in much the same vein for years. School, helping at home and the free time all children have to follow their own pursuits. Cyril would wander in the area with his friends, particularly going to Beeleigh, a local beauty spot through which runs the canal and the river. Over the Blackwater was a viaduct carrying railway lines. The structure was a hundred feet above the wide stretch of the river and boys were attracted to this place,   like iron filings to a magnet, as it represented danger to those who dared cross it. Cyril and his chums were no exception.

"Bet you won't walk across there on the parapet," one of the boys taunted Cyril, "Go on then, I dare you."

The rest of them joined in, "Yes, go on, we all dare you." They wouldn't try it themselves, but took delight in daring others.

"Bet you're afraid."

"I'm not afraid, I just don't want to," he told them.

"There, you are, you are afraid, cowardy, cowardy custard," they continued to taunt him.

That was enough. A coward Cyril was not and he proceeded to show the others how wrong they were. He was half way across on the parapet when it dawned on him that the gusting wind or a slight slip of the foot could send him hurtling to certain death in the water below. At this, his confidence fled and his fear-frozen mind could not command his legs to take another step. Terrified, he felt the sudden impulse to jump from the parapet. He could hear the shouts of the other boys, who wondered why he had stopped. The wind distorted the sounds, but he knew they were jeering; then he heard the word 'afraid'.

"I'll show them," he thought, his mind taking over again and he reached the other side, triumphant, but with legs turning to jelly at the realisation of what he had done. Feeling sick from the strain he collapsed on the grass, but he had proved he wasn't afraid to take a dare.

There were other cheeky pranks he took part in,

accompanied by his friends, such as mounting the footplates on the side of horse drawn cabs, a tempting opportunity to have a free ride. Carts up and down the High Street unsuspectingly carried many children to and from school. For the few who spotted their unwanted passengers a crack of the whip, followed by a few angry words, was sufficient to send them fleeing.

The King's Head Hotel owned a smart cab drawn by a pair of fine, black horses, often used to ferry customers to and from the Great Eastern Railway Station in Maldon. Journeys such as these had usually been uneventful, until the day when the horses, for some unknown reason, took fright and bolted. The pull on the reins, the shouts of "whoa, whoa", only seemed to increase their speed. On they raced in terror, with their ears flat against their heads, their shiny black coats lathered in white ripples of sweat. Terrified pedestrians ran from the thundering hooves. Eventually several quick-thinking fishermen, suspecting the horses might turn into Church Street, threw into the road some heavy boat chains they had close to hand, which had the desired effect of bringing the horses to an immediate halt. Fortunately the cab had been empty at the time, only the driver suffered from shock.

My father spent only a short time at All Saints' School in Maldon, not a particularly happy period, as, like many others, he was intimidated by the ruling hand the Head Master, Mr Marchant, who too readily dished out strokes of the cane and threats that made the boys shiver in anticipation. From there, his parents sent him in 1915 to the Maldon Grammar School, then fee paying, where the majority of the pupils were from families whose parents were in business. Father spoke little of this period, but, while researching the time, I heard from Len Cooper, who had been a pupil there with my father. His letter read   I have been handed your newspaper cutting concerning your I have been handed your newspaper cutting concerning your biography of your late father, Cyril Osborne. Although I have been handed your newspaper cutting concerning your biography of your late father, Cyril Osborne. Although he and I attended Maldon Grammar School, we were to have little contact until we found ourselves playing on the same side in a House football match. We were defending a one goal lead and, in the dying moments, our opponents launched a determined attack on our goal, encouraged by their supporters' shouts and yells from the touchlines. From the edge of the penalty area came a thunderous drive. As goalkeeper I had left my line, hoping to narrow the angle, but their shot was deflected wide of me, yet still on target. Then from nowhere it seemed, among pounding feet and loud gasps of breath, Cyril had appeared and launched himself in a horizontal dive across the face of the goal. His head made perfect contact with the ball and the match was won. Many years later, when the BBC *Down Your Way* team visited Maldon, Cyril's choice of music was Acker Bilk's rendering of 'Stranger on the Shore'. I have only to hear that tune and the magic of Cyril's diving header in that school day football match of so long ago, comes floating back. Good luck with your biography.

I appreciated that letter and thought how touched Father would have been to be remembered in this way.

Nellie & Jim Rivers in 1934

CHANGING TIMES

The first World War had brought with it changes affecting Cyril's family, as it did so many others. Both his brothers, being considerably older than him, went to war. Ted was posted to Salonica, where he contracted malaria, which almost killed him, and he did not return home until a year after the Armistice. Cliff was sent to France and had not been there long before he was wounded. While going over the top a piece of shrapnel caught him in the thigh and, as he fell with the wound, the butt of his rifle hit him in the groin causing a rupture. He was then sent home, unfit for active service.

The war over, Pop bought a car hire business and his two eldest step-sons, now out of uniform, worked as drivers. The car was taking over now, although there were plenty of horses still in use. This was evident by watching the steady flow of horse drawn traffic climbing and descending Market Hill, the steepest incline for miles around. Handlers with loads too heavy to manage hired the services of a work horse to pull the goods to the top of the hill; the cost was only a few pence, well worth the price.

The car hire business went well until the day Ted took some passengers to Chelmsford and only charged them the single fare instead of for the round trip. The atmosphere resulting from this error became charged and caused Ted to leave the family business. Later, Cliff set up in his own car hire firm, but not before a number of other local drivers. Competition became cut throat, so he then decided to become a publican, carrying on the family tradition.

By this time Pop was finding the business of hiring cars far less profitable and he decided to look for another means of extra income. This opportunity came one evening in the public bar of the Rose & Crown, when Pop listened with interest as he heard several of his customers discussing the forthcoming sale of the Maldon Crystal Salt Company.

On 15th April, 1922, Pop and his wife, Nellie Eliza, officially signed the document making them legal joint owners of the Salt Company. Also included in the purchase was the freehold field known as Salmon's Granary Field, "situated in the Parish of St Peter in the Borough of Maldon aforesaid, containing one acre three roods 10 perches or thereabouts, together with the shipwrights' ways, warehouse, stables and other buildings erected and built thereon". Further extensive details were listed on size and location, finally mentioning "all that brick fronted messuage" (dwelling house and out buildings), all for the sum of £1,000. Ernest Emery Brown, the previous owner of the Salt Company, had lived in the house until his death on 26 November, 1921. Under the terms of his will his wife, Alice Emily Mary, and Frederick Patrick had been appointed Executors and, under instruction, had sold the salt business and other assets in accordance with Mr Brown's wishes.

Pop, now a salt and soda merchant, had been wise when he had agreed to employ Arthur Thorogood, a former employee at the Salt Works when under the ownership of Ernest Brown, for Arthur had become a craftsman in the art of saltmaking, a skill in which Pop had no experience.

The vacancy for a driver was filled by Ted, previous grievances temporarily forgotten. He drove an old Ford lorry recommended to carry up to one ton, but which was often put to the test and loaded with one and a half tons.

Arthur had moved into the tied cottage for a Salt Works employee and it was outside this cottage that Ted decided one day to park his lorry and go inside for a cup of tea. It was unfortunate for Ted that Pop happened to be passing at the time and noticed the lorry standing idle; aggravated by this he jumped into the cab and drove away, thinking to himself, "What a bloody waste of time, stopping to drink cups of tea". When Ted came out and found the lorry gone he rushed straight to the Rose & Crown, where he found Pop rolling barrels of beer into the cellar.

"What's the idea of taking the lorry?" Ted raged.

"You should know the answer to that," replied Pop.

The conversation became explosive and Ted walked out, feeling humiliated; it was many years before he and the family were re-united.

The time had come for Father to leave the Maldon Grammar School, which today has not only changed its name to the Plume School, but also its teaching methods in accordance with today's fashions: gone is the strict discipline imposed by the old Grammar School, as Father would recall – "They knew how to knock you into shape if necessary and we were all the better for the experience". His days there had been happy.

Now to decide on a career and, as he had always had a love and understanding for animals, Pop thought this was a good basis for training to be a veterinary surgeon.

As a small boy Cyril had found a thrush with a broken wing and nursed it back to health. It became so tame it practically lived in the house; when it did venture outside it always returned to roost on the picture rail in the sitting room, much to his mother's annoyance.

"If it must stay here, I wish you would house-train the thing," she said, half-jokingly, as she knew how much the bird meant to him and she never insisted that the bird should leave the house. The bird met an untimely death when Basil King, Cyril's cousin, visited, bringing his bull terrier. Cyril was proudly showing the thrush's capabilities: at the command of a whistle it would leave its resting place and fly down to his outstretched arm, but, just as the bird came into land, the dog jumped up and caught it in flight. Too late, after the death of the bird, the bull terrier was banished from the house for ever.

23

Cyril had a small black and white terrier called Spot, who was very loyal to his owner, with almost human instincts. As boys will always be boys, Cyril did his share of 'scrumping' in an apple orchard. The owner caught him and was about to administer a clip round the ear when Spot appeared, although he had not set out with the boy. Baring his teeth and growling, he sprang at the man, who immediately released the culprit.

"I'll tell your mother when I see her and, should I catch you again, I'll more than clip your ears," he shouted.

Cyril ran from the orchard with Spot at his heels, excitedly wagging his tail, delighted to have protected his master. What worried Cyril was that his mother might be told of his wrong–doing, when she would not have hesitated to punish him and, while he would have acknowledged he deserved it, sometimes the punishment was more harsh than the misdeeds warranted: he would rather she didn't learn about the apples. Only a short time before he had had his ears boxed for playing truant from music lessons.

Although he enjoyed playing the piano by ear, he wasn't interested in reading music and playing elementary pieces. His mother had first noticed his talent when she heard him playing popular tunes on the tea room piano; believing he could become an accomplished pianist she sent him for lessons. Each time he waved goodbye to her, with music tucked under his arm, Cyril's mother had no idea he was not going to his tutor. It wasn't until one day when the teacher handed him an envelope addressed to his mother that she discovered the truth. The bill, as Cyril thought, turned out to be a letter asking why the boy had not been attending his lessons regularly. Cyril admitted that, had he known the contents of the letter, he would never have given it to his mother, sparing himself punishment.

Another incident that made an impression at an early age was, when a schoolboy, he had been playing in the salt works yard. He stayed longer than usual, past his tea time, waiting to see the small punts that crossed the river from

John Sadd's timber yard to the salt works – a short cut saving the men time and shoe leather, for which privilege they paid sixpence a year.

It was winter and already dark, when he first saw one of the punts about to cross the river. He waited for them to arrive, shivering while the cold wind made eerie sounds as it whistled into the surrounding old buildings. The lights from the factory were just sufficient for the boy to watch the progress of the punt. Without warning, a freak gust of wind capsized the tiny craft, sending the startled men into the river. There was a thrashing in the water, followed by cries for help. Cyril ran for assistance.

Arthur Thorogood, first on the scene, waded into the water and dragged the first exhausted man on to the shore, swimming close behind the second man – but where was the third? A frantic search began. It was difficult to see a figure in the water and the current was strong. No one took any notice of the little boy watching, praying for the man's safety. The man had been unable to swim and his workmates had been powerless to help him. Eventually the body was found, carried into the salt works and laid on the floor. A nearby doctor had been called and made every effort to revive the drowned man; when his endeavours failed he covered the body and left, expressing his sorrow.

It was some time before Cyril was noticed in a corner of the building with tears running down his face; he had not wanted to see or hear, but his eyes had been drawn to the body. Arthur put his arms round the boy and took him back to the Rose & Crown. It was some time before the vision of the man's face faded from Cyril's mind and longer before the nightmares went away.

My father was always more interested in the past than the future and would often start a reminiscence by saying, "Just so you can appreciate how strict my mother really was in those days, I was a teenager at the time, not that age mattered, for she made it clear to me one day by saying, 'If you are as big as a church and living under my roof, you'll do as I say.' This rule I respected, but the point

25

I really wanted to make is, I happened to be standing on the path opposite the Rose & Crown, waiting for the Chelmsford bus, when I heard mother rapping on the window, beckoning me back home. I shouted back, telling her I couldn't come as I would miss the bus; it made no difference, I had to return home.

"When I got inside the house I asked her what the trouble was; she didn't say a word, just pointing to the gloves that I had left lying on the table. I knew there was no point in saying anything further. I picked up the gloves and quickly put them away in the drawer – and made damn' sure it never happened again."

The conversation would often drift back to Spot, regarded as a member of the family. On one occasion Spot was circling the old corn bin in the warehouse, apparently anxious to get at the contents, sniffing and yapping. What did he want? Cyril wondered and lifted the lid to peep inside to see a large number of rats scurrying through the corn. Quickly he snapped back the lid: Spot looked at his master, then at the bin. Knowing what the old dog wanted Cyril lifted him into the bin and then wished he hadn't, the bin shook from the activity going on inside, together with squeals and yelps. After the noise had died down, he nervously opened the lid, expecting to find Spot torn to pieces by an army of rats. Instead, he found, to his great relief, the dog, panting from exhaustion and with a scratched and bleeding nose, but clearly the victor, surrounded by 32 dead rats. To mark the dog's courage and remarkable triumph, the rats were strung in a line across the yard for all to see and his feat was the talk of the town for weeks. A real marvel was that little dog!

APPRENTICE DAYS

Still thinking he would train as a vet, Cyril researched the field more thoroughly and was dismayed to find that he would be 26 years old before he could qualify – that seemed too long to wait. So something else had to be worked out and, although there were not too many openings for a career in those days, that of electrical engineer seemed to have a future.

John Sadd & Sons, an old established firm well-known in Maldon for their saw mills, realised the potential to supply electricity to the population of Maldon and replaced their old steam power plant, installing two Crossley wood refuse gas plants in their works.

The sawdust girls, as they were called, drove a horse and cart round the factory yard collecting off-cuts and sawdust from the saw-mills to feed the two gas plants, each feeding a horizontal low speed engine coupled to a generator. John Sadd was among the first in the country to use this method of generating electricity, which was used to run the machinery and provide lighting throughout the factory. So successful was this that it wasn't long before overhead wires were erected to carry electricity supplies to the whole of Heybridge and Maldon.

Under the circumstances it seemed appropriate that Cyril chose John Sadd & Sons to begin his apprenticeship. For this privilege his mother paid the company £50. The books necessary for his studies were a further £50, plus the added expense of a correspondence course with International Correspondence, Ltd., in London, costing £25, which Cyril paid from his own pocket. At the end of the course he qualified as an electrical engineer with 96% pass.

He then laboured seven days a week on shift work, some of the shifts involving all night working; for these long hours he received ten shillings [50p] a week. He was given one day's holiday for each year worked with the firm, so, to qualify for a complete week's holiday, one had to work there for seven years. Bank holidays, including Christmas day, were all working days. It was expected that you perform that service, no matter how long the hours.

The shed where he worked was where he ate his sandwiches at meal times on a table covered with newspaper where the log sheets were kept on which he recorded the meter readings every 15 minutes. No rules existed about comfort at work! To emphasise the poor conditions, my father spoke of the toilet arrangements, three minutes walk away. The lavatories, sited on the sea wall, were merely boarded compartments about the size of a telephone kiosk, with inside only a bucket, which often overflowed. During the summer months a clothes' peg on the nose would be an asset, while in the winter the north-easterlies would blow off the river, enough to freeze your hide; but what else could you expect when the places were so open, giving the occupant little or no privacy from the prying eyes of workmates passing by. Either way, in any weather, it made sure that no one wasted any working time there. Nobody complained for there was no one interested enough to listen to the men's grievances; you either worked amicably in the existing conditions or you left your place of employment – it was as simple as that!

Safety regulations were minimal and it was a very hazardous occupation, as Cyril found to his cost. Before the river was reinforced it frequently overflowed its banks and it was on one of these occasions, when the battery room flooded, causing the wet batteries to give off poisonous gases, as well as being an obvious danger. The town was plunged into darkness and the men's safety was ignored as they worked to restore the electricity supply. Pools of water on the floor were commonplace: the men would stand in a wheelbarrow placed in front of the switchboard to avoid the water – and electrocution – when they had to operate the switches to boost the electricity supply.

Cyril was inserting a fuse one day, just as he had many times before, when there was an almighty explosion and 500 volts burnt through his hands. The skin sizzled off, leaving them raw, and his shirt and jacket sleeves burst into flames. He was rushed to hospital to spend many weeks with his hands completely bandaged. Unable to use his hands at all, he depended on the nurses to do everything for him and tried to joke with them to hide his embarrassment at the more personal services.

For many weeks he was unable to work, but received no compensation or apology as the firm refused to admit liability. There appeared to have been no explanation for this explosion and Cyril was deeply puzzled, turning the matter over and over in his mind without arriving at a solution. Many years later a workmate on retiring solved the mystery by saying to my father, "If it's any consolation to you now, Cyril, the explosion was not your fault. We found later a D.P. switch had been left in, and when you inserted that fuse it shorted. You are lucky to be alive with 500 volts going through you. But as you didn't come to any permanent harm, we decided not to say anything about what really happened. It would have cost us our jobs." That was a bitter pill to swallow, but he found some comfort in knowing the mistake had not been his.

One Christmas Eve, when all the lights were burning and the shops were open to catch the last customers, the High Street blacked out, as if to tell shopkeepers to close their doors. The electrician foreman, Ted Galley, in charge of maintenance, had not expected to be called out on this night to climb ladders and had already started to celebrate Christmas a little early.

"Cyril, old chap, do me a favour and get up this ladder."

Against his better judgement, father climbed the

ladder, up the 40 foot pole. He knew the dangers of electricity to the unprotected, but still went ahead to tackle the job without the precaution of wearing rubber gloves. He was a bit of a fatalist: whatever will be, will be, rubber gloves or not.

"God, I'm going to cop a packet here if I'm not careful," he thought, removing the cartridge fuse and inserting another. There was a puff of smoke and a hole appeared in his pullover, then, as if by magic, the town was lit up again.

"Good old Cyril Osborne," crowed Ted Galley. "You've done a bloody good job there. But don't tell anybody you did it, mate. The job was really my responsibility and I should be in dead trouble if they find out."

He gave my father a few more complimentary pats on the back.

"God bless you, happy Christmas," and he turned for home. Father never refused to give a helping hand, even when it turned to his disadvantage. So he never gave the game away.

Cyril Osborne in his days with the Maldon Rowing Club

30

MALDON ROWING CLUB

Father was a dedicated member of the old Maldon Rowing Club in the late nineteen twenties, one of the others being Freddy Stratford, son of a Maldon shoemaker. Freddy, while studying at London University, was well-known in his college for his ability at rowing which earned him the place of skipper of his college crew for whom he rowed numerous events on the River Thames. For a period Freddy neglected his studies, channelling all his energies into the sport he loved, which caused great disappointment to his father who worked long and hard to keep his son at university. Shamed by this, Freddy made a great effort to concentrate on the forthcoming exams and his efforts were rewarded by a pass. Eventually his love of sport took him to Trinity College, Dublin, where he became a rowing coach. By this time his father had every reason to be proud for, long after leaving the college, he was still remembered, for two of the boats were christened *Stratford 1* and *Stratford 2*, an honour indeed.

For a man with such a love of boats it was inevitable that he should row for his home town, along with Bob Wood, Sidney Pond, Reg Cooper and my father, to name but a few. Those mentioned made up one of the main teams, for they were keen and prepared to practise.

The Club was fortunate to have such men as Freddy, Alf Sadd, a very capable member who acquired his skill at Leys College, Cambridge, and Steve Fairburn, who had originally taught his own style of rowing at Jesus College, Cambridge; this latter, known as the Jesus Style, was adopted by the Maldon Rowing Club to be practiced throughout their rowing days. Had it not been for the disadvantage of tidal waters drastically cutting down their practise time, they might have won a great many more races than they did. On many weekends and Bank holidays during the summer months the Club called upon the services of Rolf, for he was able to offer the cheapest form of transport; his small bus proved to be the ideal vehicle on which to strap their boat and take it to the River Stour at Sudbury, the Orwell at Ipswich or the Yare in Norwich, where various regattas were held during the season.

The Stour was one of the rivers that tested their skill for, in parts, it was too narrow for two boats to row abreast. To overcome this obstacle, a race known as the bumping race was introduced.

The maiden race in one regatta embarrassed Cyril as he stood watching with several more serious members of the Club. Full of confidence, the Maldon crew, four plus the cox, started to board the light craft. Immediately their inexperience was clearly visible, for the boat shook under their clumsy tread as they positioned themselves in readiness for the race. The fourth member suddenly ended all chances of a start, never mind a win, for his foot missed the centre plate, catapulting the crew into the water as the boat turned turtle and sank, leaving the men to scramble to the shore. Questions were asked as to who they were, but father and the rest just walked away pleading ignorance, not wishing to be associated with such a fiasco.

There were other good, capable chaps in the Rowing Club, but those earlier mentioned were those father rowed with and he found enjoyment in their company. There were those that paid their subs, but preferred dry land, the blazer, badge and social life offered by the Club giving sufficient satisfaction. The subscription was five shillings to join, plus ten shillings and sixpence [52½p] the annual fee. For those unable to afford the lump sum it was possible to pay by instalments.

"I'll never forget," father reminisced, while he gathered

his thoughts and smiled to himself. "That was a night, that was, it all started as a simple rowing practice. We should have taken notice of the warning signs, for the time, the tide and the weather were against us. Already heavy black clouds that raced across the sky had started to darken the murky waters, churned by the wind that swept unimpeded across the open marshes.

"Nine o'clock that evening, governed as usual by the tide, the four of us with Alf Sadd as cox, set off from the promenade shore. Just time enough for a short practice before the weather breaks, was the general opinion of the crew. The oars spliced through the water sending out a fine spray, soaking our thin white singlets. It didn't take too much effort to send the boat along at a cracking pace, for the wind was in our favour.

"We drew alongside Osea Island pier. Alf suggested we go ashore and have a cup of coffee with an acquaintance of his, Mr Bunting, who owned a farm on the island. It seemed a good idea at the time. We lingered over coffee, talking about this and that, until we realised how dark it had become outside. We left in a hurry and raced to the shore. As we tried to launch the boat the incoming tide, assisted by the strong wind, repeatedly tossed the boat back to shore.

"Tired and drenched from the struggle, we started to row for home, the pull of the oars seemed useless against the head wind. There was little or no conversation in the boat, only apprehension for the two non-swimmers, their fate appearing predictable at that moment, for the wash from the waves was spilling into the shallow twenty-six inch beamed boat. How much longer could we keep the boat afloat before it became full of water? The darkness obliterated our vision making it difficult to assess whether, in fact, we were on course for the shore. When at last we got a glimpse of twinkling lights from Heybridge Basin the relief was enormous, this gave us renewed energy to row to the promenade.

"It was midnight, with the tide low in the river, before

we knew for certain the drama was over. We stepped out of the boat, half full of water, into feet of mud, grateful to be alive. We looked in dismay at the boat, remembering how many fetes and draws it had taken to raise the forty pounds to buy this particular boat which had once belonged to one of the Cambridge colleges, built by Banham originally for use on the non-tidal Cam. So tight were the Club's finances that it was recorded in the Minute Book that, at the time of the purchase, there were insufficient funds available to canvas in the bow and stern projections. Three pounds was all that was needed.

"It took time to relieve the boat of her heavy load of water, but the damage had already been done, several of her planks had been strained. We all received a 'rollocking' over the affair, but fortunately the Club found sufficient money in the kitty for the repairs, after which the boat was as good as new. We had learnt our lesson, always respect the water and that goes for you and Clive," father stressed, "the river may look calm enough, but there are some dangerous currents; I have seen it take several lives in my time!"

Father had much to tell of his rowing days – 'the good old days', as he always referred to them.

"As I have said before, we were never able to practise enough, so Reg Cooper, Treasurer at the time, negotiated for the rights to row on the nearby Chelmer Canal; being fresh water we would be able to row at any time. We waited hopefully for a favourable reply, but when the answer came from the Chelmer Navigation Board, it was to say that they regretted our request had been turned down on the grounds they feared damage to the canal banks. I really took that as a personal insult to the Maldon Rowing Club. I had never heard such a load of rubbish."

"I remember the annual Club dances were always referred to as the Armistice Ball, being so close to the anniversary. Reg and I were usually roped in to decorate the Parish Hall, where today the Post Office stands. It took some decorating for it was a large area. Coloured paper chains, baubles and boat oars decked the Hall. It seemed all ready for the crowd who would shortly surge through the door for the dances were always popular and always drew a large crowd.

"On one occasion, without warning, heavy storms overhead suddenly caused a power failure, leaving the Hall and the rest of the Maldon community in darkness. Reg and I determined the show should go on, so we locked the hall door and searched for other forms of lighting. We hurried down to the Promenade, where we were fortunate to find several fishermen still working on their boats. At first they were reluctant to part with their hurricane lamps, but, having heard our story, some of them were persuaded to let us have one or two of their lamps. Carrying these and a bundle of candles we went back to the Hall.

"After having lit the lamps and candles, the power was restored and on came all the lights. I had a few words to say about that wasted effort, but it gave the other members a good laugh and I was known as the lamp lighter for some time after that.

"Dances were different in those days; one incident that comes to mind was when poor Freddy went up to a young lady and politely asked her if he might have the next dance. She curtly replied, 'I don't think we have been introduced'." Father smiled, "Freddy's reply was unprintable.

"Going back to rowing, I remember how proud I felt at the time when I won a medal as cox of the team. I wonder where the medal went to?"

There was no time like the present to start searching for it and mother was pleased it was found before the whole house was turned upside down. The small metal symbol that had given him the honours lay tarnished among some old momentos. Pleased with the find, father polished it with vigour, restoring it to its former brightness.

"We often used to sit on the river bank late at night after a rowing practise and have a sing-song to the strumming of a banjo."

As I looked at father, I could see he was re-living that

time and enjoying every minute. He went on to say, "I had a good voice in those days. Your mother always said if there had been as many opportunities in those days as there are now, I may have made a career in that field."

Mother, who had been listening, said, "That's right. I remember clearly when we were on our honeymoon, some-one in the hotel heard you singing and asked if you were a professional."

I always appreciated father singing the old songs, but found it aggravating when he imitated my voice whenever I sang, saying, "Child, you are tone deaf." He was right, but I didn't like being told so.

He never could understand my taste in music. The sound of Elvis Presley forced him to cover his ears, complaining of the racket. For father there was only one person who could sing and that was Bing Crosby.

The happy rowing days for father and his colleagues were coming to a close, for Freddy had already gone to Ireland; Alf, now a missionary, was called to the Gilbert Islands in the Pacific Ocean, which fell into enemy hands in World War II. When Alf was ordered to walk on the Union Jack he refused, this refusal cost him his life and in his twenties he was martyred for his bravery.

The carefree days were over, others were called to serve their country, while those who remained carried out essential jobs and generally kept the country running.

FATHER LEARNS THE HISTORY OF SALT

When father wasn't rowing or taking part in other sporting events he would go out and about with his friends. One day he was out walking on the Promenade with his close friend, Eric. "He was one for the girls, was Eric," said father.

"Come on, Cyril, let's follow those two girls!"

Father was reluctant. It was nearly teatime and his mother was insistent on punctuality for meals at the Rose & Crown. "Come on, Cyril, we shan't be long," Eric was persuasive. They followed the girls, catching up with them.

"Haven't we met somewhere before?" They all knew they hadn't, but that has long been the introduction used to forge an acquaintance.

"That was the luckiest day of my life," my father was never tired of saying. "The day I met your mother."

That meeting was the beginning of their courtship. Once and, sometimes, twice a week, father would ride his old motorbike fifteen miles to Great Waltham to see Sylvia. The journeys were not without hazard: more than once he landed in a ditch when the road was foggy; drenching rain chilled him and gave him bouts of bronchitis; snow caused him to skid, injuring his leg – "But it was worth all the discomforts, just to see your mother!", father assured me.

It was during his courting days that Cyril developed a very bad cold on the night he was to meet his fiancée. It would never do to appear with a streaming nose and all the attendant discomforts. People relied on remedies unlike the magic pills to be obtained today. Eucalyptus was one which, when sprinkled on to a handkerchief, helped to relieve nasal congestion. Cyril never did anything by half measures, being always under the impression that double the dose cured the ailment in half the time. Needing a quick nostrum he laid on the bathroom floor and dispensed several drops of eucalyptus from an eye dropper into his nose; the results were quick, but not in the way he had expected. Pain, such as he had never before experienced, filled his head, temporarily blinding him. As time wore on the effects wore off and his senses returned to normal, much to his relief.

The episode did nothing to destroy his belief that a double or even treble dose of medicine would cure anything quicker. All through his life, unless we watched closely and often this did not make much difference, he took his medicine in larger doses than prescribed. The more he took, the quicker the recovery, so he thought.

It was during this time that Pop said, "Cyril, have you ever thought of going into the salt business?"

He answered truthfully that the idea had never occurred to him. Thinking further about it, the more he liked the idea. He realised then that being an electrical engineer was not going to satisfy his ambitions – it was just a job. So he made up his mind to change.

Pop was pleased; he was getting on in years and would like to hand the management to a member of the family. Not that Arthur was unsatisfactory; on the contrary he was an excellent workman, looking after the business as if it was his own.

Pop never forgot the time when he saw a light in the Works late on a Sunday night. Cautiously he investigated, wondering if there was a trespasser inside or if Arthur had left lights burning. "Hallo, anyone there?", Pop's voice echoed through the quietness.

Arthur was somewhat startled by the unexpected visit, so Pop questioned him, "What's all this then about working on a Sunday night?"

"Just getting ahead for Monday morning, Mr Rivers."

Arthur was appreciated, but the many extra hours he

worked were rarely reflected in his pay packet, for the tied cottage where he lived was considered to be the extra bonus. The business could not have borne the strain of having to pay out hours of overtime, in any case.

So Cyril knew that if he joined the firm he would not be getting anything easy. Pop would expect him to do his share and more, whether he was family or not. Arthur was pleased and looked forward to teaching Cyril all he knew about the business. Another pair of hands would help lighten his and Pop's load. So started Cyril in the Salt Works, on long hours and a low wage that was barely enough to support him and his newly wedded wife.

His mother had had a house built into which they moved. They called the house, built on lands adjoining the Salt Works, Sylvia Villa. It was easy enough to get to work – too near for a conscientious man, as it meant he spent untold hours seeing that everything was going right.

Cyril learnt the history of the salt works and its ancestry. According to legend salt was first manufactured in Maldon two thousand years ago, when the Romans ruled Britain. Cassius Petrox was Commander of the Legion stationed at Maldon and he disliked the fog, the damp and the cold winds that swept across the open marshes to the camp. This caused his bones to ache and he only found ease from his pain when bathing in the warm sea water his slaves prepared for him. After such a bath he could march with his men through the wild countryside. The water for his bath came from the salty river Blackwater and was heated in the bath from a fire made underneath. One day the Legionaire was late returning from his march and the slaves had kept the fire going to heat the water, not wanting to incur his wrath if he arrived back tired and aching, unable to take his hot bath. So late was Cassius that the water had been kept at boiling point, too hot to use and he was as angry as if the water had been cold.

Then he noticed the small white crystals at the bottom of the bath. When he found that these were salt crystals and that his slaves had inadvertently discovered the method

Inverted-pyramid shaped Maldon sea salt crystals

of producing salt from the seawater, he was full of praise. He sent samples of the salt to his brother officers, who asked for more. Demand increased and the slaves were told to make more salt, as much as possible. The excited Cassius resigned his post as Commander and devoted his time to salt making. This was the very beginning of Maldon Salt as an industry.

Salt was then very highly valued: the word 'salary' derives from 'salarium', the money given to Roman soldiers to buy their salt. So high in estimation was salt that one's place at table, above or below the salt placed there, signified a person's social status. From the value of salt came the phrases 'Worthy of his salt' – meaning that he deserves his success – and 'He is the salt of the earth' meaning the very best. Salt means life, as essential to our bodies as the air we breathe. Totally deprived of salt, we would surely die. The salt composition in our tissues has been found to be similar to that of sea water and thought to be an evolutionary survival of 270 million years ago, when the migration began from sea to land.

The next documentary evidence of salt producing at Maldon was in the Domesday Book of 1086, which listed 45 salt pans in Essex, four of which had belonged to King Edward the Confessor. The industry flourished throughout the Middle Ages, despite being heavily taxed. In the time of the Tudors and Stuarts salt was stored in heavily barred cellars called girnels, only opened in the presence of customs men.

Salt making, like other ancient industries, has left a record in some of the field and place names of today. Salcot, a nearby hamlet at the head of Salcot Creek, certainly had at least one salt-cote, where salt was made: 'cote' is a small shed for housing or making anything. Along the many creeks and inlets on this coast there are fields showing that salt works formerly existed there, such as Home Salt-coates in Stow Maries; Salcote Stone Field in Tollesbury; Salt-acre Marsh in East Mersea; Salt-cote Marsh in Burnham. The Salt-Acre, Salt Field and Salt

Pasture are all well inland, at Roydon, High Easter and Barking, probably named after some abnormal saline deposits found there.

Salter's Piece in Sible Hedingham, situated far inland, is probably named after a former owner named Salter, due to an ancestor who had been a salt maker. It should also be noted that the inn name 'The Three Cups' or 'The Cups' occurs five times in Essex, at Harwich, Great Oakley, Colchester, Maldon and Springfield, representing the armorial bearing of the Salters' Company.

It seems that this part of the Essex coast offers greater facilities for making salt than any other part of England. There are many extensive shallow and narrow mouthed estuaries, creeks and inlets through which the sea flows. Salt is deposited in large quantities by evaporation on the mud flats and saltings surrounding these places and this salt is taken up in solution and re-deposited by each tide, twice every twenty-four hours, thereby making the water exceptionally salty. From this daily occurance over the centuries the marshes have become heavily saturated with salt. As rainfall is usually lighter on this coast the water salinity is greater here than anywhere else in England. It is not surprising that nearly all the Essex salt works were not on the open sea coast, but on the shores of the estuaries and inlets.

In his will in 1497 John Beriffe the elder, merchant of Brightlingsea, left, for the purchase of two bells for the parish church, 'one hundred marks which William Bounde and Robert Barlow owe me for one lot of salt'. In 1501 Henry Boode, of Burnham, left his house to his wife, except 'the berne [barn] in which my salte lyeth' and a new shop with an inner chamber wherein more salt lay and he directed that she was not to meddle with these until the salt was out of them. In 1547 John Creke of Hockley, describing himself as a 'weller' (by which he meant a salt boiler), left to his son, Thomas, his 'salcotte and leddes belonging to the said salt house, with all other implements that a weller ought to have, but no salte; by 'leddes' Creke meant, no doubt, leaden evaporating pans. His salt cote was most likely on the estuary of the river Crouch.

On Whit-Sunday, 1532, when the Heybridge church wardens made a play and a feast they paid twopence 'for a peck of whyte salte' - probably locally made.

About 1710 a bill relating to the salt trade was before Parliament and a return was made of those places where salt was then made in England. From this it appears that, in Essex, salt was made or refined at Manningtree, Colchester and Maldon, the refiners all using water borne coal for boiling their brine pans.

In 1785 a writer spoke of the demand for 'the famous Maldon Salt' and another in 1823 described Maldon as 'famous for its salt'.

There was a firm of salt makers, Bridges, Johnson & Company of Heybridge, when John Bridges was the owner of 'very extensive works'. These were near Colliers' Reach, near to Heybridge Basin, on marsh still referred to today as Salt Court, but it seems to have gone by 1823.

About this time, Robert Worraker, described as a 'salt maker', residing in Heybridge, had probably bought Bridges' business. Later, he or one of his descendants appears to have removed his works to Fullbridge on the opposite side of the river Blackwater. He carried on his small, but dwindling, business until 1882. Finally faced with either closing down or selling, he chose the latter, disposing to T Elsey Bland of Maldon, who pursued the business with increasing success, trading as the Maldon Crystal Salt Company, the deeds of which are still in existence.

In the 19th century salt making went into decline due to the heavy taxes. By 1805 the tax on salt had risen to £30 a ton, which created so much public resentment that in 1825 the tax was abolished, when the sales of salt rose rapidly. As a result the industry in Cheshire expanded and the markets were flooded with rock salt and coal. Dealers panicked and sold their salt at less than cost price. This was disastrous for the industry and forced the majority of salt manufacturers to cease trading, never to re-open.

Today only six remain in the United Kingdom; the Maldon Crystal Salt Company being unique in that it still produces sea salt using the same process handed down by generations of Essex craftsmen.

The Company has been famous for many years, from the time it was noticed that the crystals had a unique formation. In an article published about the business in 1880 the crystals are described as extremely curious objects – thin, white, shell-like, quadrangular at base, rising in the shape of a pyramid with a truncated cone. In size they vary greatly, some being as much as two inches square; others are equally perfect, but no more than one-eighth of an inch. The form is invariable, but the size seems to be determined at the commencement of crystall-isation and, after a crystal has started to form, it does not grow. One of these salt crystals forms the Trade Mark of the Company.

It seems fitting that salt crystals with such an ancestry should come from the town of Maldon, the history of which stretches back to Roman times. In the 5th century the Legions left Britain and, in their place, came large numbers of Angles, Saxons and Jutes, warlike people. Maldon was then called Maeldune, meaning the hill with the cross – a vantage point from which to discern the onset of unwanted company, for their approach would be clearly visible as their boats left the open sea to glide down the narrow estuary of the Blackwater, flanked by deserted marshland.

By August, 991, England was constantly troubled by Scandinavian invaders, causing destruction, murder, rape and looting. Angered and determined to defend their territory, Brihtnoth, Ealdorman of Essex and his followers trapped a party of Danes who had occupied Northey Island, accessible only at low tide by a 400 yard causeway to the mainland. As the tide receded the invaders started to cross the causeway, Brihtnoth's men being in a strong position had the advantage of picking the enemy off as they came in almost single file. As the story goes, the Danes saw defeat and begged to be spared until they could reach the mainland, where they could fight on equal terms. Unbelievably Brihtnoth agreed to this request, only to be slain with many of his followers in the battle that ensued.

On 7 October, 1171, Henry II granted the earliest extant Royal Charter to the Borough, acknowledging the status, independence and privileges that the town had enjoyed since Saxon times.

Buildings erected in the Middle Ages are recorded in the Borough's *White Book*, housed in the archives. Many are still standing today: All Saints Church and vicarage, the Moot Hall, Beeleigh Abbey, the Blue Boar Hotel and the protected ruins of St Giles, once a leper hospital.

During the 18th century Maldon's trade flourished, largely through her sea port. The opening of the Chelmer – Blackwater Navigation in 1797 also brought further business to the town, as did the opening of the railway from Witham in August, 1848.

In Maldon father found all he ever wanted. Proud of her heritage he would often say, "There's no place like Maldon" and, although he had travelled to many places abroad, he would always return saying, "The best part of going away is coming back."

Maldon Crystal Salt Company's works before modernisation

FATHER ENTERS THE BUSINESS

The responsibility of fostering the traditional salt industry in the same manner as his predecessors was the task that faced my father. These were the lean years of the recession and profits were low. He could not modernise the works without money, nor could he afford to engage extra help. He said, "There were times when I wondered was it worth carrying on, but I was never afraid of hard work; my philosophy was 'if there is work to be done, get on and do it'."

He lived by that and later, looking back on his life, said, "No workman today would do what I had to do then."

Pop lent a hand when he could and the making of salt went on against all odds. Arthur took pride in teaching Cyril the craft of making Maldon salt – there was more to it than he had at first thought.

It was not necessary then to make salt every day: it was manufactured against orders received. There were two salt pans in operation, each filled with 500 gallons of sea water and heated by coal fired furnaces. Making salt at one point is similar to making jam for, at boiling point, any trace impurities rise to the surface as froth and are skimmed off. The heat is then reduced, allowing the water to simmer and evaporate. At this stage inverted crystals, many linked together, start to form on the water surface. In slow motion they sink to the bottom of the pan, letting other crystals form on top. The complete process takes up to 24 hours, until most of the water has evaporated, leaving a pan of salt ready to be harvested.

It would seem to the layman a simple, easy process, but the salt maker knows different. The salt content of the water varies according to the weather conditions and tides. He has to have the 'feel' that all is going well, together with technical knowledge. The coal fired furnaces were always hungry, burning six to seven hundredweight of coal during each saltmaking process. There were no thermostats; the only aid Cyril had for regulating temperatures was a damper, a large metal pendant hanging from a chain, with which he raised or lowered the heat. His expertise in operating this became second to none. The texture, size and whiteness of the salt crystals depended on the correct temperatures being maintained, together with the 'know how' secrets, which he said were kept under lock and key.

It takes 500 gallons of water to fill one of the salt pans, so when the spring tides arrived once a fortnight the storage pool was filled, for only the spring tides are suitable, for they are then at their deepest and saltiest, after having washed over the large expanse of salt encrusted marshland, giving the high salinity required. Only the middle channel is suitable, for the heavier salt water flows closer to the sea bed.

These high tides very often arrive at an inconvenient time, meaning that Cyril had to leave his bed in the early hours of the morning to stand on the river bank, chilled to the bone, to make sure the pool was filled. Every time this happened he wished the spring tides would come at a more acceptable hour. It was then that he welcomed the warmth of the kitchen, still with a few remaining embers glowing from the fire. As he arrived back home at daybreak he would make himself a cup of tea and smoke a cigarette before returning to bed for a few hours.

The sea water in the storage pool was left to settle for a couple of days, then pumped into concrete storage tanks, where it would undergo a careful filtering process before being finally pumped into the malleable steel pans, gushing from large taps.

The salt makers
David Footman transferring salt to the dehumified store room

There was never any need to wonder what to do first in the morning at the Salt Works. The furnaces had priority for without the fierce heat the salt making process would never begin. As the furnaces had to be stoked fairly regularly a variable mountain of coal and dust stood near-by, ready to be shovelled in. As the heat built up it was conveyed through an intricate system of flues and baffles to create even heat underneath the pans.

During the burning of coal the heat would fuse the residue together and it was these hot lumps, still giving off sulphur fumes, that had to be raked out every morning. Armed with a long metal rake Cyril would clear out the hot clinker and rattle out the ash. By the time the second furnace was dealt with the air could be blue with sulphur smoke, making him cough continuously. It could have been disastrous had he eaten his breakfast before 'clinkering out'. "It's a wonder I've got any lungs left," he would gasp after these bouts of coughing. Then he would light up the furnaces for another day's work.

On notification that a delivery of coal had arrived at the railway station yard Cyril and Arthur would take the old Ford lorry early in the morning to fetch the 70 tons of coal waiting to be unloaded in open trucks. If they started early enough they might move ten tons a day. As it was loose they first had to put it into bags, many weighing as much as two hundredweight. The bags were then loaded on to the lorry and taken back to the Works, where they were unloaded and carried into the stokehold.

Cyril stood on the pile as it mounted, taking the bags from Arthur, emptying them ever higher until the coal reached the ceiling. Planks of wood were fitted in to stop the loose coal rolling back. This meant three handlings in the day, making a day's work some 30 tons.

The chafing from the sacks of coal left my father's back raw and painful. The next day, to alleviate the pain a little, he would strap a hessian bag filled with straw across his back and carry on working. All this suffering was to save about one shilling and sixpence a ton, as loose coal was a bit cheaper, and also to save demurrage of two shillings, charged by the railway if it was not unloaded within a stipulated period. It was not meanness that prompted these savings, although they were considerable in the days when money had a far greater value, but the tight budget on which the business was run that forced these economies.

Another of the unpleasant jobs was to clean the flues running under the salt pans. Cyril detested it, but it had to be done to ensure that even temperatures were maintained. To gain entry he had to crawl in through the furnace door, only eighteen inches square.

An even dirtier job was moving the coal dust and slack, used for damping down the furnaces, from the trucks. Father dressed for the job, wearing an airman's old leather helmet and goggles and a thick scarf wound round his neck, looking more like a pilot of the Royal Flying Corps than a salt maker. No matter what defences he took against the black dust it still found its way all over his body, taking him days to be rid of all traces of it.

Before father took over the works a belt-driven pump was used to raise the water from filter bed to storage tanks, which meant that someone had to stand on a wooden platform working the handle up and down relentlessly and monotonously. The job lasted all morning, sometimes longer. The leather belt working the flywheel needed continual repair as it split frequently. Pop swore that one of the workmen put grit on the belt making it wear and break when the task became too much for its operator. Whatever the cause, it gave my father much aggravation in repairing or replacing it. Getting a replacement to fit was the biggest problem, until father had a proper pattern made; then, after soaking the leather in water, it was a perfect fit. Shortly thereafter the hand pump was dispensed with and an electrically operated pump was installed.

Now Arthur was beginning to feel the strain of the heavy work he had been used to all his life. He wore a wide leather belt to control a hernia, but would not ease up or see a doctor. "I'll be alright," he would say, whenever Cyril

50

showed concern for his health. "Plenty of life in the old dog yet."

But father wasn't convinced, knowing how ill Arthur really was. Then suddenly he died of pneumonia. Father was stunned. Not only had a good and honest workman gone, he had lost a loyal friend. Would he be able to replace Arthur? He never did.

One or two men came and went. No one, it seemed, could fit in quite as Arthur had. Father did employ one or two who were 'worth their salt', but as time went on it became increasingly more difficult to engage staff to work as father did, for times were changing. Then came Les Numan, six feet tall and strong, a likeable character. He settled well into the Salt Works for a few years, until the urge to travel became too strong and he joined the Navy.

A suitable replacement would once again be difficult to find, as father knew from experience. An advertisement in the local paper attracted only a few applicants, none of whom father felt were really suitable. However, after much deliberation he decided on Tom Brown. Father's hesitation in choosing him had been solely due to the fact that he did not look strong enough to do the heavy work involved in the job, for his appearance was delicate and his face pale and thin. "Damn' good worker, never known him to be ill," was the opinion of his previous employer.

After hearing this recommendation father felt confident he had made the right decision. Tom's looks belied him, for he stayed strong and healthy, working hard throughout his many years employed at the Salt Works. Personalities were sometimes in conflict, for Tom had his own ideas on how he thought things should be done and, at times, resented father correcting his ways.

Apart from the hard work and the long hours that father put in at the Salt Works, there were all sorts of calamities to contend with. There was the problem that winter could bring, when the fresh water in the river would reduce the saline content to such an extent that it was not profitable to make salt, the yields being so low. Some winters they

Tom Brown bagging and weighing Maldon Salt into 1cwt bags

would not attempt to make salt for weeks. It appears that not only do you 'make hay while the sun shines', but also salt. The tides of winter, swollen with fresh water, would wash over the banks into the yard, flooding the lower part of the Works by two or three feet, making working difficult, as well as unpleasant.

It was an advantage at times, being in the salt business, to know in advance how the weather was going to behave. In order to master this knowledge, Cyril started to study the phases of the moon, wind and tidal conditions, known to be connected with the weather. He became so expert at reading these signs that he was seldom wrong in his daily or long range predictions.

Father was determined at times during the winter to battle against nature and produce salt, which would always turn out to be a long and laborious task. At half hourly intervals through the evening to past midnight the pans would 'set over'. This meant that the crystals, though formed, refused to sink in the normal way, but formed a sheet on top of the water, forcing father to continuously splash the scalding water with a long wooden spatula, encouraging the crystals to float to the bottom.

Father hated to admit defeat and close the pans down, but this did give an opportunity to do repairs to the old building. There was no money to spare to call in workmen. The beams supporting the roof over the pans were bowed with age and from the weight of the pantiles, which were specially placed to allow the rising steam to escape from the simmering pans. The odd beam, unable to bear the strain, has, on occasions, hurtled into the pan. The brick wall at the back of the furnaces also bowed alarmingly from age: that too had to be repaired and shored up.

It was when repairs were being undertaken beneath the salt pans that an interesting discovery was made. Digging down, they unearthed ancient brickwork turned to solid rock by salt water. Was this proof that Cassius Petrox had started his salt works on that very same spot on the edge of the Blackwater? The County Archaeologist could not confirm that the remains were Roman, probably that they were late medieval. Confirmation that salt production had taken place under the same roof for many hundreds of years, if not thousands. It was this long tradition that kept father going in the hard times. How could he give up now?

Some of the more unpleasant maintenance jobs that had to be done when the furnaces were not in operation were not for the claustrophobic or the work shy. Flue cleaning was one of these and it was through lending a hand that Pop came close once more to losing his life. To reach the flues under the salt pans he eased himself through the 18 inch square door of the furnace. It was a tight squeeze, with his cleaning equipment, a long pole with a spade shaped piece of wood at the end on to which was tied a cleaning rag. He, like my father, was a heavy smoker and, especially on an uncongenial job, would puff away at a cigarette. He was doing so on this particular day and, when he had smoked it to the very end, believing that he had stubbed it out, threw it into the soot in the flue. Almost at once the soot ignited, sending out choking fumes. He managed a cry for help and father, nearby, heard him, rushed to the furnace door and desperately pulled at the protruding pair of boots, which was all he could see of Pop. He was carried into the fresh air where, under a sooty covering, Pop's face was a ghastly white, for he realised how close to death he had been. He recovered, but never again found the courage to go through the furnace door, the job falling to father or Arthur.

The pantile roof had its disadvantages. While allowing the steam to escape, the wind could blow the smuts from the tall chimneystack through the openings. It was disheartening to see it drift into the pans or on to a pile of freshly raked salt from the pans, after all the painstaking work involved to produce a pan of salt. There were also occasional complaints from neighbours about the thick black smoke that periodically belched from the stack when the furnaces were stoked. The grievance was usually about the smuts deposited on washing as it flapped from clotheslines in the breeze by the water's edge. The Salt Works was not the biggest offender, for John Sadd, timber merchants on the opposite side of the river, also came in for criticism when the smoke from their factory appeared to be in competition with the salt works. Visits from Council officials failed to find a solution until some years later with the introduction of the Clean Air Act, when smokeless fuels were used and solved an age-old problem.

There was no official teabreak at the Works in the early days, so father would take a break when it was convenient. After they were married, mother would take a mug of tea into the Works for father. One winter's day she called to him in the yard, "I've left your tea on the side of the pan. Drink it now or it will be cold."

Father drank a sip or two, intending to drink the rest later, but he was unlucky, for that day the temperatures had dropped so low that the tea had frozen in the bottom of the cup. It could get very cold in the Works when the furnaces were out, for there was no other form of heating.

When the salt crystals had been raked to the side of the pan they were collected with wooden shovels and put in large wooden bins nearby, where it remained for several days to drain. The brine water that slowly dripped from the salt was collected into sump holes especially made for that purpose. This liquid was called 'bitten' and was supposed to have strengthening qualities. It was seeing that that sometimes reminded father of the time when, as a boy, he had heard a customer remark to his mother, "You don't look well, Mrs Rivers, working too hard, I wouldn't wonder." She ignored these comments, considering them to be personal. No one seemed to have noticed her increasing weight, for she always had a large figure over which she wore loose silk dresses, so it was amazed customers who learnt the news on the evening she was absent from the bar that she had just had a baby girl.

Viola was weak from birth, doctors doubting she would survive. At the age of two she could barely stand or walk. Father could remember the relentless fight that went on to restore her health and that 'bitten' from the Salt Works was used to some effect. It was collected from the sump holes in a stone jar and added to the child's bath water. For a time she gained strength in her limbs, but then lapsed into a coma and died. This was a tragedy for both parents, but especially for Pop, for she was his only child.

Father recalled too, when the salt was still far from dry, it was put into sacks, then taken to the old black boarded warehouse in the works yard. In the warehouse the first floor was used for storage. On the ground floor was a large brick oven, inside were brick ledges into which fitted copper trays. A fire burnt inside the oven, creating the heat needed to finally dry the salt, which had been spread on the trays. Father spent hours turning over salt with a small wooden shovel allowing the steam to escape. When sufficiently dry, the salt was once more sacked and taken to the Rose & Crown, where it was spread out on the kitchen table. There was no need to weigh the salt for as much as possible was packed into the cardboard drums with a tin bottom and lid that held about 12 ounces, although no weight was stated on the bold mustard coloured label. The black lettering on the label announced 'The Maldon Pure Table Salt' and underneath was the trade mark, a pyramid shaped salt crystal. The analysis, clearly printed, was a selling point. Dr Hill Hassell, a well known writer in the *Lancet*, showed his faith in the product by giving permission for his declaration to be printed below the analysis that, "From these results it is evident that the Salt is of unusual purity and very carefully prepared (signed Dr Arthur Hill Hassell". He later wrote a detailed article in the *Lancet*, about the salt, saying the "Maldon salt has no bitter aftertaste noticed in the salt used for ordinary culinary purposes. We have no hesitation in recommending it for household use, for it is pure as well as attractive".

Later, an easier method was found for drying the salt. As the bricks round the pans retained heat for many hours, the salt was put into hessian sacks and stood against the brickwork. They had then only to be turned occasionally to dry all through. If the salt was too wet when put into bags it dried in hard crusts, making it difficult to handle.

Customers liked the large crystals for culinary use, so father's aim was to produce the largest possible, meaning a lengthier process and costing more to produce.

It was this aim to put the customer first that often gave him longer working hours and not always to his gain. He would go out late at night without a grumble or, if he did, it would be a silent complaint, after an urgent request from a butcher or baker who had run out of salt.

He remembered times when he was called from his bath to load a waiting vehicle and he travelled miles to take one bag of salt to oblige a customer, not taking the loss of profit into consideration.

As time passed only the largest crystals were packed for sale in the shops as the finer salt was sifted out. A copper sieve, 18 inches in diameter, was used; an arm aching job, shaking until only the largest crystals remained. The packing changed to a thick parchment coloured box giving it an old-world look, the black lettering still confidently claiming, "The only Pure Table Salt". No weight was yet stated on the packet. They packed as much in as the box would hold. Twelve boxes on a grocer's shelf could have a different amount in each, the majority weighing about two pounds. Customers took delight in handling each, to claim the heaviest.

While Maldon Salt was made for culinary purposes and salting down meats and fish, father also purchased from I C I granular salt for water softening and crushed rock salt used for defrosting purposes in icy weather. Several lorries would arrive during the course of a month each carrying 20 tons. They unloaded and carried the 400 bags, each weighing one hundredweight, into the warehouse. No one grumbled at the hard work and it seemed not to tire them at all.

WORLD WAR II

When war broke out in 1939 the main shortage in the family was time. The Salt Works consumed most of the hours in a day, the Rose & Crown the remainder. Father's mother, now known as Nannie, was no longer able to manage as she had done in the past and Pop's increasing attacks of asthma forced him to bed on occasions. My mother helped in the bar and father lent a hand when other obligations allowed.

He was not called up as his work as a salt manufacturer fell into the category of an essential service. As a contribution to the war effort he volunteered for ARP duties. The drills were held in the Territorial Hall at the corner of Silver Street. When matters of importance had been dealt with and the nights were quiet the men played darts and chatted.

Time did not mean a great deal to father in the sense that he did not watch the clock. If there was something to be done at the Works he did it and was usually so immersed that time flew by and he was often late for duty at ARP Headquarters, with a genuine reason – 'the furnaces needed damping down... the pans were 'playing up".

He was briefed on how to use a rifle and what to do in the event of an invasion. "It's basic common sense. I've been rabbit shooting; I can handle a shot gun. If there was an invasion, I'd know what to do."

"And what would you do?" enquired mother, who had been listening to him.

"I'd sit on the beach and pop the enemy off one by one as they came ashore," he said. We all knew he made light of the things that really worried him. He would keep things bottled up, so as not to bother us. When he joked and laughed, it may have seemed that he put his head in the sand, but this was not so.

The men of the ARP carried out their practice to deal with possible invasion at Beeleigh. The only foe they encountered was the farmers' enemy – the rabbit. Father, while taking a break from manoeuvres, was warned not to smoke near haystacks. A more serious side came one night when he was sent on a mission to deliver a telegram to another unit 15 miles away. In a crisis it would have been essential for information to be delivered quickly he was told. So the powers that be wanted to know how long it would take. He set off on a motorbike into the dark night. During nighttime the countryside was in complete darkness, unless lit by moonlight and to show a light was a chargeable offence as it could have helped enemy aircraft locate a target. Lights on cars and motorbikes were reduced to a mere slit by having a cover fitted and were really very little use. Father rode at a snail's pace. All signposts had been removed and there was nothing to guide him. His legs became frozen and seemed detached from his body, while his mind was numb from the strain of searching for clues to guide him on his mission. Eventually he turned back in despair, only to find Headquarters locked and the men gone home, tired of waiting for him.

War brought its tragic reality to the town: bombs dropped in Washington Road, demolishing several houses, killing some people and injuring others. Father was called out and gave first aid while waiting for the ambulances, and tried to give confidence and help to relieve the stress of the victims. He talked very little of these experiences. There were a couple who were very lucky in this incident. They were in bed when the blast from the bomb blew them, complete with bed, from the house, suffering nothing worse than surprise and shock.

On another occasion father was called out after a German 'plane was caught in the searchlights. He watched it, caught in the rays like a moth trapped by light, until it was shot down in a ball of flame, spiralling to earth. One of the wings broke away and splashed in the river outside the Salt Works, yards from our house. The pilot had parachuted from the 'plane, but was found dead entangled in a tree.

Later in the war came the doodle bugs, officially called the V1s. We used to watch them from an upstairs window as they jetted across the sky, clearly visible with their fiery tails. They would pass the house and disappear towards the marshes. Then, one evening as we watched, father said, "We are safe while they keep going; you only need to worry when the engine cuts out." As if it heard him speak, the rocket passing the house, went silent. "Down," was the only word father managed to shout before the explosion shook the house, rattling the windows. The next day we learnt it had made a large crater in the marshes.

When the siren announced a forthcoming air raid we usually went down the outside steps to the cellar under the house, where we felt comparitively safe. With hindsight, it might have been an illusion, as we could have been flattened under tons of rubble. This occurred to father, so he bought a Morrison shelter, a massive steel contraption, rather like a wire cage with a reinforced steel top, its size practically filling the dining room. We slept in it only a few times during air raids as it was too claustrophobic. The most useful aspect of the shelter was the top, on which a number of things found a resting place, as well as being a stage on which my friends and I danced and acted.

There was a brick shelter built at the Salt Works, but we didn't want to go there at nights. When the siren sounded father always said, "No need to panic, there's plenty of time." Mother would call on him to take cover, while he stood and scanned the sky. "Looks as though London is catching it again tonight."

"Do come in," mother tried to persuade him.

Still he seemed calm as he assured us, "You don't think

they are interested in bombing Sylvia Villa, do you?"

Mother, feeling nervous, reminded him about Washington Road.

"Ah," he would say, "that was obviously off course."

"Off course or not, it could happen again."

To that father did not reply.

Nannie and Pop had an air raid shelter built in the small orchard at the top of the Rose & Crown yard. Deep down below the earth's surface workmen built a reinforced concrete shelter, fitted with bunk beds and stocked with tinned food enough for a siege. Eight steps led down to the access. They must have found peace of mind just by having it there, for no one ever entered the door seeking shelter throughout the war. It was nicknamed 'the tomb', perhaps leading Nannie and Pop to think that anything was better than being buried there.

There was a robbery at the Rose & Crown. No entry was forced, as the back door was never locked, as it led to the bar as well as the living quarters. The burglar had gone upstairs into Nannie's bedroom, also unlocked, where he forced a locked drawer. It wasn't until the following morning they found that about £500 was missing, a great deal of money in those days. Detectives were called in, but failed to find the culprit. After several weeks had passed there appeared little or no chance of recovering the stolen money, until a Commander at the Langford military base telephoned the police to say that his suspicions were aroused by a soldier asking two or three times a day if his leave had been granted. This was odd as his wife had followed him from camp to camp and was living nearby in a small cottage. The man was spoken to, but gave nothing away. The police, still not satisfied, visited the cottage and told the woman that her husband had been interviewed and they had reason to believe a parcel had been hidden in the cottage. Turning pale, she went straight to the chimney and took out a parcel still wrapped in the original brown paper taken from the Rose & Crown. The soldier was tried and found guilty, being sentenced to a term of imprisonment.

Things had a habit of disappearing from the Rose & Crown during the war, although no one could pin down the culprits, for the most part. However, the finger of suspicion was pointed towards some people who had taken up residence in a condemned cottage in the town. They had the opportunity, for they were cleaners at the Rose & Crown for a short time, but nothing was ever proved.

"Do you know, Sylvia," father said to mother, "the bar was full of darkies tonight." He was referring to the coloured American servicemen stationed at nearby Birch aerodrome. "They must have a thirst, they'll drink anything that resembles alcohol. I don't know how their stomachs put up with it." Pop sold everything he had, even some old bottles of wine he'd kept in the cellar as curios since before 1912. They were covered in dust and cobwebs, although they could have been all the better for keeping. He might have been dubious about serving them in the ordinary way, but the Yanks were pleased. Anything for a bottle, apparently.

Father could never understand how anyone could acquire a liking for alcohol; he had never been tempted himself and, when persuaded to have a drink socially, took it like medicine, straight down without tasting.

Birch aerodrome was never completed as an airbase and was mostly used as a hospital, but the presence of American servicemen in the district made many a landlord better off.

Cigarette stocks, however old, were brought out to combat the shortage. "Got any fags, guv?" was the usual question to Pop over the bar. One day he surprised everybody for, instead of shaking his head, he said, "Yes, I'll sell you some 'Robins'." These were snapped up and smoked, the customers unperturbed that the paper was stained yellow from age and the tobacco like chaff.

During the war with food on ration father, while delivering salt to a few local tradesmen, was able to buy the odd grocery line or, sometimes, even meat, helping to eke out the rations.

A year before the war ended my brother, Clive, was born, which, for father, completed his idea of a happy family. He could not think of anything more that he wanted and, in his eyes, we were quite perfect.

The end of the war was celebrated with bonfires in the streets, fuelled by any old mattresses, furniture or wood. The fires burnt until the early hours and the worried looks dissolved from the faces of the people in the town; they celebrated as if there was no tomorrow. Things would be different – and so they were, but not as they had expected.

Father saw the change: "In our family it was noticeable. No longer could maids be engaged to work at the Rose & Crown, as before, when they were expected to rise at 6 a.m., clean out the fire grates, wear white caps, frilly aprons and black stockings for less than five shillings a week, with one afternoon off a week and answering meekly, 'Yes, ma'am, no, ma'am," always trying to please for fear of losing their jobs. There was more money to be earned elsewhere."

The Salt Company's Works today

FAMILY INCIDENTS

There came a time when mother expressed a wish to learn to drive. Father wasn't at all keen on the idea for he had just purchased a smart new black Vauxhall, one of the first to roll off the assembly line since the start of the war and he also failed to see the need for her to learn to drive. It was still an age when women drivers were in a minority and could cause many a laugh amongst the menfolk. Mother was not to be deterred.

Invariably I was in the back seat when mother took the wheel, a witness to events. Father, usually long suffering, was now the instructor and acted out of character by being irritable and impatient when mother jerked the car in a series of bunny hops when starting off in first gear. When she crashed the gears that was too much to take, "I can tell you now, Sylvia, you will never make a driver."

The times mother threatened she would never drive with father again!

However, the time eventually came when he decided she should take her test. "I've taught you all there is to know, the rest is up to you."

Mother, on first meeting her examiner, was asked, "Do you have your insurance papers?"

Flummoxed by the question, she answered, "I don't know, my husband deals with that."

"You shouldn't tell me that," he replied.

Having regained her confidence, she was then under instruction to drive away from the kerb, beginning her test. She signalled with her right indicator, as she had always been taught.

"Don't use your indicators, Mrs Osborne, I now want you to give only hand signals."

"Hand signals," mother repeated, for father had never told her about hand signals, in fact she had only ever used indicators.

Undeterred, she started giving the requested signals, but, at times, found it inconvenient, for her two hands seemed busy handling the steering wheel and changing gear. The examiner was not pleased by her three point turn, taught by father, when she used the kerb as a stop on which to rest the wheels before moving off.

When it came to question time, father hadn't instructed her on the Highway Code. She didn't need the examiner to tell her that she had failed, but, when she told father, his only comment was, "Some are born to drive and some will never drive."

Mother determined to prove him wrong, corrected her mistakes, and passed her next driving test.

It was some time before mother started to drive on a regular basis, for she was often called to the Rose & Crown for, although Pop and Nannie still worked hard, age was taking its toll and not being able to employ maids as before was hard on them. Nannie could not relax her Victorian views, which would not allow her to be familiar with servants. Kind and fair she would always be, but 'familiarity breeds contempt' was her dictum.

This meant mother spent many weekends helping at the Rose & Crown without much appreciation from her mother-in-law, who considered it her duty. There was never much rapport between the two. Mother said that if she wanted a favour she would ask Pop: when she did, it was to borrow his car. He replied, "If I want it smashed up, I can do that myself." She didn't see the twinkle in his eye and it was much later before she did borrow it.

Perhaps Pop was thinking of the time when his car did get smashed during the Great War. A Zeppelin had been brought down in the Goldhanger area; of course, everyone who was able went to view it. Pop drove his car along the narrow lanes, when suddenly there appeared a large gleaming black car, driven at speed. Pop slowed down and drew over to the side as much as possible, expecting the other car to do the same as the road was so narrow. To his amazement the other car sped on as if he wasn't there and tore off the wing of his car as it passed. He was even more surprised to see the Royal Standard on the bonnet of the other car, but the chauffeur looked neither left nor right, with the King sitting in the back of the car. Pop could only gaze from his wrecked car as the Royal automobile disappeared without stopping.

Time off was still scarce for father, but one memorable day he promised to take us to Stansted Gymkhana. Before we went to the show ring to view events we wandered round the sideshows on the outskirts of the field, among them people bowling for a pig. Father fancied his chances and paid sixpence to the jolly man who was shouting, "Come along, ladies and gentlemen, try your luck."

The wooden balls all scored well and the man was impressed. "Very good, sir, can I have your name and address, please. A score like this could be the winner."

I looked at the little pink creature, circling his pen, occasionally squealing. Other people were looking at him too, doubtless seeing him as a potential Sunday dinner. I couldn't bear the thought of that. During the afternoon I went two or three times to see what the highest score was. Father wasn't optimistic, but at 6 o'clock he was declared the winner. We were a little bewildered at becoming owners of a baby pig with no idea what we were going to do with it. I believed that father's idea was to fatten it up and have a good few Sunday dinners of pork, but I didn't ask, fearing it might be true. Things have a way of not going as planned: so it was with the pig. He was called Stansted and became a member of the family. He was given a stable to himself where he thrived. As he grew at an amazing pace, so did his appetite. Our baker saved all his stale bread and cakes, while mother cooked vast quantities of potatoes, together with anything else edible, in an effort to satisfy Stansted.

Full grown and 'fat as a pig' he became uncontrollable. He routed up the concrete floor of the stable. Then he would push his great bulk against the door, which gave way, letting him into the field where he ran amuck, chasing my terrified pony, who lashed out in terror. It would take hours getting Stansted back into his stable. Father grumbled about the time wasted over the freedom loving pig, but did nothing about it.

Then came the time when father did question Stansted's future. "What are we going to do with him, we just can't keep him any longer. Marvellous, isn't it? I thought he would end up as our dinner. It's damn' ridiculous, I know, but I couldn't bear that. I'm quite fond of that old pig."

Eventually Stansted was sold to a butcher in another town. We did not eat pork for months, just in case a bit of Stansted had found its way back to our butcher.

Talking of Stansted reminded father of the time he bought a dozen chickens from old Tom. "Once again, I was going to fatten them up, intending to have a chicken now and again for dinner. They roamed around my field laying eggs everywhere. I never had the heart to kill any of them. They eventually popped off one by one from old age."

There were times when he was given a brace of rabbits or a pheasant for dinner. Immediately he passed these over to mother for preparation for the oven, for he was unable to bring himself to skin a rabbit or draw poultry. "If I do that I shall never eat it," he would say.

"That is all very well," said mother, who was not that keen on the job either, "but what about me?"

"Well, if you cannot do it, my dear, we shan't be able to have them. It's as simple as that!" So this unpleasant task was always left to mother.

Stansted had left a gap in the family or so we children felt and it didn't take much persuading to convince father that this was true. "I'll speak to your mother," he said, "about having a dog; after all, she will be the one to look after it."

"Clive and I will look after it," I promised father.

"Yes, I know all about that, but the dog still needs looking after when you two are at school and the responsibility will fall on your mother's shoulders."

The idea of having a dog brought back mixed feelings to father for Buddy, a wire-haired terrier, the first family pet, had been playful and subdued within the family, but once away from his own territory, developed a vicious streak, attacking and killing chickens and some prize rabbits. Father was temporarily able to satisfy the owners by paying for the damage Buddy caused, but when he jumped at a passing cyclist, tearing his trouser leg and sinking his small, sharp teeth into his ankle, that was another matter.

The police, now familiar with Buddy's activities, thought the time had come to take action. "Either you have the dog destroyed or we shall bring a Court case," warned the constabulary. These words hit father like a stone, for he was very attached to the dog, but there was no way out.

"It's no good crying, my dear," he told me, "we just couldn't keep Buddy. He is far happier where he is now; he has gone to a farm where he can chase chickens all day and do what he likes." I must have been very young, for I was satisfied with the explanation and it wasn't until much later that I found what had really happened to Buddy.

This time father chose a Golden Labrador for their temperaments are such that there would be no chance of her disturbing the peace outside her territory. As a puppy she caused unimaginable damage in the house, chewing her way through several expensive books, taking the heels off shoes and fingers off gloves, and nearly killing an apple tree in the garden by stripping it of bark. Several times she came close to being expelled from the house, but, after endless reprieves, she settled down to become one of the family; intelligent, gentle and obedient, for father trained her well.

She loved us all, but had a little extra affection for

mother. Wherever mother was, the dog wasn't far away. She was called Sandra and if she could not find mother, she would search for her in the shops, never failing to find her wherever she was. There was less traffic in those days and therefore she ran free, with little risk of being run over, except for one day when she saw mother on the opposite side of the street and dashed across to greet her just as a car was coming. There was a screeching of brakes and mother covered her eyes from the pain of seeing Sandra injured or dead. Seconds later a wet nose nuzzled her legs and she felt the swish of her tail, Sandra had survived unscathed.

A bitch should always experience one litter, so father sent Sandra away to be mated to a fine looking pedigree Labrador. When her time came father sat up for several nights with Sandra, finally assisting her as she gave birth – to twelve dogs and a bitch! The story was carried on the front page of the local paper: "Is this a record?" – we never heard to the contrary.

Thirteen puppies were too many, the vet suggested seven would be sufficient for her to look after. Several were given to caring hands, who were carefully instructed about the feeding, milk every hour or two through an eye dropper. Mother, with her hands already full, took on the job of rearing one of the puppies, called Barley, who became very strong and healthy.

It took father longer than usual to find caring homes for all these pups. Not all prospective purchasers were fortunate enough to buy a puppy, for if father had any hesitation in believing the hopeful owner was unsuitable, he wouldn't sell to them. Money was secondary to him, the puppies' future was more important. It was a wrench on all our hearts each time one was sold, only Sandra seemed to benefit from the decreasing numbers; by the time the last puppy left she had had enough of the strain of bringing up a family.

She died at the age of 14; it was like losing a member of the family for she had brought us all a great deal of happiness.

Father loved animals, especially dogs. I think he expected the same treatment from them as he gave, mainly a healthy respect, so that when he obliged a doctor by delivering a bag of salt to his large country house, he went to the tradesmen's entrance, where, to his surprise, a large black dog attacked him. The doctor called the dog off, too late, blood was pouring from father's hand. The doctor apologised, "Sorry about that, come in. I'll put some anti-septic on it. Don't worry, the dog has a clean mouth."

He seemed unconcerned and did not even mention the torn shirt sleeve caused by his dog. "You should not have any trouble."

This was not the case for, as he drove the lorry home, father's pain and swelling increased. At home it became still worse and a doctor was called, who was very concerned when he saw the hand. After questioning father and learning what had happened he asked if the first doctor, the dog's owner, had cauterised the wound. The doctor did not seem pleased by the casual treatment previously administered, but he treated the hand and, during the next few days, father suffered a great deal of pain. Could this lead to blood poisoning or even rabies, we wondered? For the doctor's parting words had been, "Don't hesitate to contact me should you have any problems."

We all worried silently, watching him closely, terrified of the outcome. At last the hand healed and father suffered no ill effects, much to everyone's relief.

Father said afterwards that he thought the doctor's off-hand attitude was due to the fact he thought the salt was being delivered by a workman, not the owner of the business. For it was still an era when tradesmen entered by the back door and were treated as a caste below the wealthier society.

For my father there was no upper, middle or lower class; it was all one to him, treating everyone the same and not understanding why others did not do likewise.

On another occasion he was delivering salt to a large

70

country house, when a huge Alsatian rushed at him. He dropped the bag of salt and spoke to the dog in a firm friendly manner and it backed away, allowing him to deliver the salt. When the dog's owner heard about this he said to father, "Good God, man, you were lucky, he never lets anyone past these gates unless I'm here. He is very vicious, you really must have a way with animals."

Needless to say, father was very put out when he received his one and only dog bite.

Cyril Osborne and Les Numan raking salt

THE FAMILY MAN

Father was essentially a family man. His family and his work filled his life. As he said, he hadn't time for anything else. My brother and I loved and respected him and, usually, tried not to do anything to upset him. But as children do, we had moments when we were naughty. Father did not let his love for us deter him from teaching us to behave well. He was firm about this. I remember answering back in a cheeky manner when father's immediate reaction would be "Just make sure nothing like this ever happens again," which was usually enough to see that it didn't.

My father really hated discord in the family. He was very sensitive about this, but I did not realise this until I was much older and married. If I was to pass their house without calling in, father would worry that perhaps the reason might have been that he had unwittingly said something to upset me – never the case, it was only a matter of time. That was how it was with our family, we were close and concerned with each other most of the time.

It was all the more surprising then that father did not pay more attention to his own health, knowing that we should worry about him. Perhaps he thought that if he made light of hazards and ailments they would disappear. What the family worried most about was his smoking, although it was not until later years that all the dangers of it were spelt out to us. His bouts of winter bronchitis were enough for us to try to persuade him to stop smoking.

Although he rose early in the mornings, he found difficulty in collecting his thoughts, but a cup of heavily sweetened tea and a cigarette in the peace of the kitchen, while he viewed the river through the window, set him up for the day and he could then keep going until well into the night. Father maintained it was something in the air, perhaps a lack of oxygen first thing in the morning, that slowed him down.

I often heard the floorboards creak as father crept across the landing, the sound echoing through the stillness of the early hours. I also heard mother's whisper "Make sure you put your overcoat on."

Father's thoughts usually took the line, "I'll be back shortly, I can't mess about putting on a coat."

It would be pleasant enough walking to the Salt Works in pyjamas on a warm summer night, but it seemed, more often than not, that the suitable spring tides would arrive in the early hours of a bitterly cold morning. The sluice gate did not operate automatically, someone had to close it when the reservoir was full or the water would empty out again. So father waited while the tide came in, perhaps with snow falling, and the bitter north-east wind that often blows off the river in winter penetrating his clothes. He would stamp his feet and buff his arms vigorously round his body in an effort to keep warm. Then, when the reservoir was full, he needed enormous strength to close the sluice. This was a tricky operation, for the heavy wooden pole with a huge plug on the end, had to be manoeuvred into place twelve feet under the water line.

These cold and laborious jobs would have broken the health of many men. So it was remarkable that father continued his heavy work load without coming to more harm. He always insisted that his absorption of salt from the steaming pans of salt water helped keep him healthy, as well as the Maldon Salt he sprinkled liberally on his food. In his earlier years he had a good appetite. In spite of this mother and I found it necessary to continually urge him to take care where his health was concerned.

"Your hands," I've heard her say. "You will have real trouble if you treat them like that," as she found him scrubbing his hands with liquid bleach.

"Don't talk rubbish, Sylvia," he replied. "I've scrubbed them like this for thirty years and never had any trouble."

"You won't always be so lucky."

"I've got good blood that keeps me healthy," he retorted, as he tried to scrub off, at different times, the cement, paint, oil or varnish he had been using.

Mother continued to worry. "Why you can't wear gloves at work I will never understand."

"Good Lord, tell me how I can work properly humbugged up in gloves?" He dismissed the idea as unmanly.

"Other people wear gloves," she insisted, but he would never do as other people did. Mother enlisted my help in trying to persuade him to take care and not use neat bleach on his hands.

"Don't be silly, child." I was still not grown up in his eyes, though I was past 40 then. "You haven't lived yet, stop worrying, what harm do you think a bit of bleach is going to do?"

I was only too pleased to find comfort in his words. I did worry and dreaded that something terrible would happen to him if he carried on with his careless attitude towards his health.

Not that swallowing a fish bone was a careless act, but not explaining to the doctor just how bad his throat really was, for fear of making a fuss, was being irresponsible. Mother once again needed to take charge, she visited the doctor herself, requesting that he saw a specialist. Immediately the wheels were put in motion. An infected throat, badly lacerated by the fish bone, was diagnosed. The specialist sympathised, "A throat like that must have caused you a great deal of pain and discomfort."

"You could say that," father smiled, admitting for the first time just how painful his throat had been. Special medication eventually healed the wound, allowing him to eat once more.

"It wasn't as painful as when I had my eye trouble as a teenager," father started to reminisce, the thought of the pain making him wince.

"A bee stung me on the eyelid; unbeknown to anyone at the time the sting left in the eyelid scratched the pupil, setting up an infection. At one stage a Harley Street specialist warned me there was a possibility I might need to have my eye removed. After months of treatment it eventually improved, leaving me with impaired sight in that eye. This triggered off depression that lasted for many months. I remember my mother was very concerned and, when time allowed, she took me to several comedy shows in London, hoping this would lift my depression. A few years later, while still wearing glasses, I met your mother. She was convinced I didn't need them, she probably thought I looked more handsome without them," he laughed, "so to please her I dispensed with them for a time."

Mother, catching the last sentence as she came in through the front door, denied this, saying, "Cyril, I never heard such nonsense, it was you who said you could see just as well without them."

Father had a wash day once a week when the heavily salt-encrusted hessian bags were cleaned, to make them usable again. He liked to choose a windy day so that the bags dried well. The wash tub was a large metal tank filled with cold water in which he would rub and scrub the bags until they were pliable. Then he would beat the water out against the wooden fence and hang them to dry. Once again, the skin on his hands took heavy punishment. He never treated any cuts; nature did a better job, he said, and once again we were not able to prove him wrong.

There were times, however, when his actions angered both mother and me. Anger and fear for his wellbeing mixed uncomfortably when father broke his leg carelessly jumping from the tail board of the lorry on to uneven ground. The plaster cast on the leg caused much swelling and pain, because he insisted on walking about so much!

The doctor told him to rest as much as possible at first. "Rest!" father exploded, "that's about right. How does he think I can carry on my business sitting about all day?"

75

"Cyril, all I know is that the doctor has told you unless you rest your leg a little bit more, you will be out of action altogether."

Still he did not take advice and, with his usual remark, "I can't be humbugging about here all day," he hobbled off to the Salt Works.

When the doctor arrived he was surprised to find that father was not at the house. Mother apologised, "I'm sorry, doctor. If you don't mind waiting a few moments, I'll get him from the Works."

"Please don't worry, Mrs Osborne, I'll go and see him there," the doctor replied curtly, picking up his bag. He arrived at the Salt Works just in time to see my father, who had just finished clinkering out the furnaces, with his bandages ablaze, beating out the flames with a sack.

"Phew, that was a near thing," smiled father, when catching his first glimpse of his visitor standing at the door. The doctor did not smile and, as soon as he saw the flames were under control, turned to leave, saying, "Mr Osborne, I wash my hands of you." Mother was not amused when she heard what had happened.

Father had a hernia which, in the end, needed surgery. When he came home from hospital he was specifically told he must rest and take things easy for six weeks. No lifting seemed an obvious part of the recovery. Mother felt confident that she had convinced him to take care and went about her work.

Returning to the room where she had left him sitting in an armchair with a cup of tea, she found he had gone. He did not answer her call, but she could hear the sound of a broom on concrete. It came from the garage, where she found father, sleeves rolled up, cleaning the floor. He returned to the house later, very pale and overcome with nausea, glad to sit down. He uttered no word of complaint, probably knowing he would get no sympathy.

During his convalescence a customer came to the house with an urgent request for a bag of salt − which weighed 112 lb. He apologised for calling at such a late hour, but stressed it was important he had the salt as he was about to start making a batch of bread for his customers the following morning. Father never turned away business and went to get him the salt. Carrying it on his back he slipped and fell and was unable to get up again because of the excruciating pain. The man ran for help and he and mother managed to get father back to the house.

Mother was too angry and upset for words and, as father was still in extreme pain, she told him she would send for the doctor, but he asked her to wait for a while. We were worried about internal injuries, but said nothing. Gradually the pain eased and, by the next day, it seemed no lasting damage had been done.

It was strange that customers, knowing father owned the Salt Works, expected him to carry their salt, without offering to help. On one occasion he was asked to carry 10 bags from the lorry to a barn, quite a long walk, but acceptable to father, until he found he had to climb a ladder into a loft to stack the salt – even then he obliged.

He continued to fight off minor disasters, which could have become major, although he never saw it that way. Like tearing his hand on a rusty nail, another time on a rusty scythe. "Please get a tetanus injection," we begged.

"I've never had one and I'm not starting now," was his retort. "I don't know what you are all worrying about, I'll be alright." And he was!

Still he continued to smoke heavily and suffer winter bronchitis. "Stop smoking," pleaded the family.

"Don't keep on," was always the way he dismissed our nagging, as he called it. But the time came when he needed strong antibiotics to clear chest infections. For all that he never stayed in bed and only an extreme case of illness kept him from his work.

He dressed every morning as the weather dictated at the hour he got up. Whatever the change, to very cold or very hot, he would not put on or discard a garment. It was this odd habit that led him to tell me about a childhood episode. He was sweltering one day as the temperature rose. Thinking he would be pleased I handed him a glass of lemonade as a refreshment. He refused.

"I never drink the stuff, my dear, the thought of it turns my stomach. It always reminds me of years ago at the Rose & Crown when I walked through the kitchen to get a drink. There on the table was a glass full, as I thought, of fizzing lemonade. I drank three quarters of it so quickly it hardly touched the sides. Then the taste registered and I knew immediately what it was. Pop had left a glass of false teeth cleanser there, from which he had only just removed his dentures." Although father could see the funny side of most things, he failed to see the humour in that.

In spite of all these mishaps his resilience brought him quickly to recovery. "It's all that salt," he would say. "You know they send people with chest complaints down the salt mines to improve their health; that's a fact."

Each talking point could so easily lead father on to an entirely different subject, like the time he discovered a small piece of history relating to an old cottage.

He had been sheltering from a severe storm in the old stables that once housed the work horses belonging to the Salt Works. The rain continued to lash the boarding of the nearby cottage without pause. Father waited some 15 minutes until he saw the clouds break, allowing rays of sunshine to spread on to the cottage. The warmth of the sun on the wet boarding released clouds of steam. As father looked the name clearly became visible – Wang Pu Cottage. As the steam faded, so did the words and, although he searched many times, he was never again able to see the name, which had disappeared without trace. Wang Pu Cottage was apparently the original name when a family of Chinese traders lived there in the late 18th century.

This incident led father to continue reminiscing, this time about the East Station, Maldon, much talked about for one reason or another. It had been officially opened in 1884, then being popular with travellers, as well as bringing increased business to the town. Years later, as cars gave alternative means of transport, fewer passengers used the line and it was eventually axed under the Beeching Plan in 1966. The railway station had changed little since it was built and it wasn't difficult to imagine times gone by. Especially the night father and I stood in the shabby, ill-lit waiting room trying to warm our hands by an old cast iron stove choked with ashes, while we waited for the arrival of the 9 o'clock train on which my pony was travelling. The only sound was from a large faced clock that ticked noisily as the hands fell heavily from one minute to the next.

Father wiped the grime stained window with his hand-kerchief, hoping for a clearer view, but all he saw was a dark deserted platform and the beginnings of a November fog. We chatted about the day's events and, once again, I threw my arms round his neck to kiss his cheek, for I was so delighted with the pony he had bought me that day at the Cambridge Horse Sales.

The noise of the steam train in the distance roused a porter from his place of rest. Swinging a bright lantern, he flashed the light in the path of the slowly advancing train to pilot it alongside the platform where it eventually stopped amidst a noise of applied brakes and hissing steam.

The experience of travelling had upset the pony and sweat lathered his neck as he pulled at his halter rope, securing him to a bar inside the box.

"Steady, steady, old boy. There's nothing to be afraid of," soothed father, giving him a gentle pat on the neck, encouraging him from the box.

"You gonna see alright?" enquired the guard, "it's pretty dark with this 'ere fog about. You best take me lantern, I've got several more. Just make sure I gets it back termorrer."

I was pleased that father had insisted on accompanying me and the pony back to the stables for, as we crossed the bridge over the river, he reared and became difficult to manage, as he caught sight of the boats partially shrouded in fog, which he clearly thought threatened his safety, but again father's voice calmed him down.

79

Vic Dorrington and a Salt Works lorry in the twenties

The filling and inspection area

INCIDENTS

My father loved to reminisce and, as I grew older, I listened more intently and with more interest. Some of the tales I had heard over and over again.

"Have I ever told you about that?" he would say at the beginning of a trip down Memory Lane. If I told him I had heard it before, it made no difference, for I knew I would hear it again. He would lean forward as he talked and light a cigarette, drawing satisfaction from every puff. It definitely relaxed him and helped him through many business worries.

"Your mother was not always sympathetic when I was late home, especially on a Friday when I had been delivering in the Chelmsford area that was the longest journey of the week."

"What made you so late?" she would always ask.

"Well, you know what it is, what with one thing and another," he would answer.

"All I know is you could have been home much earlier if you hadn't talked to every customer."

"It's all very well for you to say that. I couldn't just dump a bag of salt and walk away without a word."

The argument would continue over the triviality for mother knew how much he enjoyed a good chat and it was usually this that caused him to be late.

Father had a naturally loud voice. Mostly it didn't bother us, but there had been some embarrassing moments. For instance, in a restaurant father would talk unknowingly to an interested audience of diners. He should have charged a fee for entertaining, as he brought many a smile to the listeners' faces with his jokes. Some, I'm sure, must have heated beneath their collars at his remarks, but he was completely unaware his voice had reached their ears.

"I must tell you about the time I was at a party with your mother. I suppose I must have been talking rather loudly while reminiscing unpolitely about an 'old flame' of many years ago. Then a tap on my shoulder made me look round. 'You happen to be talking about my wife.'" This didn't bother father at all, he just whispered to mother, "I think I should have kept quiet about that, don't you?"

Father didn't intentionally upset people, he would rather keep the peace, but he could be insistant in order to achieve what he wanted. This attitude paid off when I had been in bed with bronchitis. Continuous coughing had burst a blood vessel in my nose and there seemed to be no way of stopping the bleeding. Father got into the car and drove to the surgery. At that moment the receptionist was not at her desk so, unable to wait, father strode into the consulting room. The doctor had a patient with him and tried to send father out of the room.

"My daughter's nose is bleeding, we cannot stop it."

"Good heavens, man, I can't come right now, as you see, I have a patient. I've never heard of anyone dying of a nose bleed."

"There is always a first time," father told him.

Seeing how distressed father was the doctor asked his patient to make another appointment and came to plug my nose, saving me a trip to hospital.

Father would do anything for his children, including celebrating traditions, Guy Fawkes being one of them. I believe he enjoyed such occasions as much as we did.

Weeks before 5th November we started to build a bon-fire in the field opposite the Salt Works, helped by father who always managed to find a considerable amount of un-wanted material to make a huge pile, for he never did any-thing by halves. It would become so high it needed a ladder to reach the top on which finally to place the Guy.

"Tidy old fire you be gonna have there, Cyril,"

commented a few of the old locals as they passed nearby.

Mother was the only one who wasn't happy about its size. "It's too big. If the flames spread it could catch the fence alight."

"No chance, it's miles away from the fence," father exaggerated, for he could never comprehend such possibilities.

He had obviously forgotten the time he had made a general bonfire in the garden, when it caught the grass alight, the flames spreading dangerously close to the house. Out came the garden hose to quickly dampen the path of the advancing fire.

We waited impatiently by the bonfire with a crowd of excited friends for father to come and perform his promised duty of lighting up. There was another surprise in store for, when he did arrive, he had with him an enormous box of exciting-looking fireworks.

It took a large can of paraffin before the fire finally ignited, to burn fiercely, throwing out hot sparks forcing us to move further away to safety. The warning on the rocket type fireworks 'Do not hold in the hand when alight' were ignored by father as he struck a match and lit them in his hand before placing them on the ground where they exploded. Once he wasn't quick enough and the rocket launched from his hand, burning his fingers and leaving him most surprised at the power of the firework.

"You shouldn't hold those damn' things," came a voice from the crowd, "my brother lost three of his fingers like that."

Father didn't comment, but I noticed he started to take more care. Having lit the firework, Jumping Jack Surprise, everyone was more than surprised, for it appeared to erupt in a cascade of coloured stars, crackling and banging, sending out green and red smoke lasting well beyond the normal time of an average firework: it seemed impossible that a firework could have so many facets. It was impossible, for in the dark it hadn't been noticed that a live spark from the fire had landed in the box setting off the remaining fireworks. What a finale to the evening!

Father would look out of his window early in the morning and, in winter, would be dismayed when he saw a thick fog, screening his view of the river. He referred to such a morning as a real pea souper. Driving the lorry in fog was something he didn't look forward to.

One morning by the time he was ready to leave visibility had not improved and the lights on the lorry did little to improve his view ahead, for they were unable to penetrate through the wall of fog. Leaning out of the cab window, driving at no more than 15 m.p.h. he was just able to follow the white line for some distance before turning off on to a country road where there was nothing to guide him, apart from instinct. By dusk he had completed his deliveries, well behind schedule. His customers were pleased he had turned up on such a day for on the wireless it had been announced 'London blanketed in fog; many travel services cancelled or delayed'. It was that bad.

Fog has the tendency to confuse. Father now in the countryside he knew so well found himself completely lost. He felt the lorry climbing slowly while shingle crushed beneath the wheels – he had driven off the road on to the site of a gravel pit. As he stopped the lorry and jumped out of the cab to assess his bearings he shuddered, for only yards ahead the ground fell away into a deep pit.

Back on the main road once more, he was able to follow a car for some distance before it stopped, this time finding himself in a pub yard 5 miles from home. This wasn't to be the end of events for that day. Father hadn't seen the cyclist hugging the grass verge and had driven so close to him that the poor man, fearing being crushed, had jumped with his bike into the waterlogged ditch. Father only became aware of the near accident when the man, recovering from his fright, cycled alongside the slow moving lorry to tell his story.

After that at the mere hint of fog, father always took along one of his workmen, who on occasions walked in front of the lorry acting as a guide. During these times father genuinely had a good excuse for being late.

"Why are you so late?" mother greeted father on so many occasions.

"I'll tell you, but you wouldn't believe this, Sylvia. As you know I was delivering salt to Goldhanger Fruit Farms today and, as I drove into the yard, the foreman put his hand up to me, now what was his name? he used to work down at the wood yard in Maldon."

"Do come to the point, Cyril."

Father had the habit of explaining in prolonged detail everything that led up to a situation. He wasn't to be hurried and would tell the end of the tale all in good time.

"As I was saying, I can't think of his name right now, but it will come to me later, no doubt." He went on to describe how cold it had been in the factory, how bleak and uninteresting the countryside was in the area. By now I had noticed that mother had slipped out of the kitchen, father, unaware that he did not have her listening ear, carried on with incidental details. After several minutes mother slipped back in again, picking up the threads of the story at the point where he had entered the factory.

"Do you know, there was this damn' great heap of rhubarb, green as grass, stalks as thick as your arm, waiting for treatment and, do you know, by the time it had been chopped, cooked, coloured and canned, it ended up as slim pink sticks of appetising rhubarb, no resemblance to the rhubarb before its preparation."

Mother was now really interested and asked, "Did you just walk in or did someone show you over the factory?"

"Damn it, Sylvia, I've just told you all about that."

"Oh, yes," mother would say, pretending to remember in an effort to cover up for her absence.

Father would say to me, "I've never known anyone like your mother, one minute I'm talking to her, the next minute she is out hanging up the washing or she has just slipped up the town for something or other. She wants to be doing half a dozen different jobs at the same time, she is always in a hurry.

Mother shouted back from wherever she was, "I haven't got time to stand around all day."

"I never said you had, my dear," father shouted back. "It's just that you can never stay still, always dashing about somewhere."

The fourth Sunday in the month mother worked with father on the accounts. She did most of the office work for she had been trained in bookkeeping, as well as having the ability to carry on that side of the business, while father preferred having the production side. One of the largest accounts was usually from the local garage where father bought his petrol. As usual, when it came to be checked, father had kept the knowledge in his head.

"Did you or did you not have this amount?" mother would question him.

"Ah, if that was the day I went to Dengie I would have filled up with 10 gallons."

Then mother would become impatient. "Why don't you write down every time you fill up, it doesn't take a second."

"It's all very well for you to say that, Sylvia. I reckon I must have been in a hurry. That's if I did fill her up that day."

There were discussions, arguments, checks over records and searches for various documents. By the end of the day everything was usually in order. Father was far too busy making and selling salt; unless he was doing that he considered he wasn't working. Office work was not for him.

While searching for papers, he would unearth various letters that he would stop and read. Like old newspapers, these generally turn out to be more interesting as time goes by. Father would drift from the present to the past and quote from letters and papers any bits of information he found. On one occasion he found papers that started this train of thought.

"Marvellous when you think the Maldon salt business has been going on for about two thousand years."

"Cyril, you can't say it's been going on for two thousand years."

"Sylvia, I know more about the salt business than you."

"I admit that, but the Maldon Salt Company has not been in existance for two thousand years."

Both wanted to prove their point. Father thought for a moment, then a twinkle came into his eye. "How about you having a word with the Romans; they knew how to make salt two thousand years ago."

"Cyril, be serious."

"I am being very serious. Well, let's just say salt making in Maldon was mentioned in the Domesday Book. Which reminds me, I have deeds going way back, but the one I remember offhand was when J Felton sold the business to J Worraker in 1831. I have a little booklet that was produced in 1891 when B E Bland managed the business. I'll find it in a minute."

"Don't bother now, it's getting late, Cyril," mother protested.

Father wasn't to be deterred and kept on reading.

Maldon Crystal Pickling Salt, £5 per ton delivered.
Supplied in quantities of 1 cwt. and upwards.

For present day purchasers, the cost of one tonne of Maldon Sea Salt would be approximately £710. However, today it is no longer possible to buy in bulk quantities, for Maldon Salt is only packed in 250 and 500 gram packs.

The 8 pages of the small, smoky-green booklet, now faded with age, had clearly been published as a sales campaign to be sent to prospective customers, for existing users were familiar with Maldon Salt. B E Bland opened the first page by saying –

MALDON CRYSTAL SALT CO.,

MALDON,

ESSEX.

DEAR SIR,

We have much pleasure in forwarding you a few of the opinions of some of the London users of our **Crystal Pickling Salt**. You will notice that these are all well known firms, and that they agree alike as to the Efficiency and **Economy** of our Salt.

We shall be pleased to forward you a sample free of charge on application if you will favor us with a trial.

Yours,

MALDON CRYSTAL SALT CO.

MALDON, ESSEX.

Manager, B. E. BLAND.

By Appointment.

T. WALL & SONS.

113, Jermyn Street,

London, S.W.

Dear Sirs,

With reference to the **Salt** you supply to us, we have pleasure in stating that for the purpose of making Pickles we find it more efficacious than other Salt being much stronger, thus enabling us to keep them for a longer period : moreover being more economical.

Yours faithfully,

(Signed)   T. WALL & SONS.

Harrods Ltd.,

87 to 125, Brompton Road.

Dear Sirs,

We found the **Salt** much better than the ordinary Salt for pickling Beef, a much smaller quantity being required for a Brine. It also gives the Beef a much better flavour.

Yours truly,

(Signed)   W. NORMAN,

Buyer Meat Department.

89

JOHN BARKER & CO., LTD.   KENSINGTON,

                                            LONDON, W.

DEAR SIRS.

        It is now some months since I first
used your **Salt** for brines, and I am pleased to say
that I am delighted with the results.

        Firstly.—The marked improvement in the
colour of the meat obtained by the use of about 75 %
less saltpetre than is used with ordinary salt.

        Secondly.--The length of time the brine keeps
sweet and the absence of slime and grit, which more
than make up for the extra cost.

        I shall be pleased to show our brines to anyone
interested you may care to bring here at any time,
and wishing you well deserved success.

                I am, DEAR SIRS,

                        Yours truly,

    (Signed)   T. ROBERTS,
                    Manager Meat Department

DOWLING & SON,

        GRAND AVENUE,

    LEADENHALL MARKET.

                            TLEMEN,

        We have pleasure in informing you that
we found your **Salt** superior in every way to
the ordinary salt. We have used it for over twelve
years, and for curing purposes we can safely say it
has no equal. At first we were inclined to think it
dear at the price, but experience proved that such a
small quantity is required as to more than compensate
for the difference in price.

        Kindly forward usual quantity, and oblige.

                Yours truly,

    (Signed)   DOWLING & SON.

90

ORDER RECEIVED

6/October

1803.

SIRS,

I shall be obliged by your forwarding me by as early a carrier as possible 3 bushels Maldon Salt. I will thank you to enclose the A/c of it which I will pay you in any way you may order.

I remain,

Your obedient Servant,

(Signed)   ROBERT BARCLAY.

Results of Analysis of

MALDON CRYSTAL SALT.

	Per 100 Parts by weight.
Chloride of Sodium *(Pure Salt)*	99·617
Chloride of Magnesium ...	0·198
Sulphate of Magnesium ...	0·067
Sulphate of Lime	0·118
	100·000

From these results it is evident that the Salt is of **unusual purity** and very carefully prepared.

(Signed)   ARTHUR HILL HASSALL.

After much comment, having read the leaflet carefully, he then came across a bundle of old letters tied together with string. As he started to read these his memory was jogged at the mention of saltpetre.

"I remember taking a bag of saltpetre in mistake for Maldon Salt to old Aubrey, the baker. I didn't discover the mistake until I arrived back home. In somewhat of a panic I 'phoned him to explain what had happened."

"Don't worry old chap," the baker said, "I've already used it in the pork pies. It's not harmful, it just means that my customers will not need to take a dose of salts if they eat the pies. Anyway, thanks for letting me know. See you again next Friday."

"Marvellous what they got away with in those days. I've seen them crumbling up stale pork pies in preparation to incorporate them in a new batch."

Father always had a story to tell, an incident to relate. His memory, usually so vivid and detailed, let him down one day when he went to Court to give evidence after a lorry had damaged his car.

While driving one evening an impatient lorry driver overtook him on a narrow corner, tearing the wing off his car as it passed. It was fortunate mother was a passenger and was able to take note of the lorry's number. Father blasted his hooter in an effort to stop the driver, but the only reaction was increased speed. Without doubt it was a clear case of dangerous driving. As Maldon Police Station was only a few miles away he reported the accident and the lorry was traced, the driver appearing in Court on what should have been an open and shut case. When father was called to the box he answered the questions confidently, but tending to embroider on the incident. The defending solicitor, noticing these little aberrations, questioned father again and again, confusing him with words, so that he contradicted his statement. It ended up with the guilty driver getting off scot free and father fortunate not to have been jailed. His solicitor was baffled and could only comment, "We must have been talking at cross purposes."

Nellie & Edward Osborne, with Ted and Cliff, about 1900

RELATIONS OF THE PAST

I had always thought of life as a never ending cycle, many changes, but never ending, until Nannie died two weeks before her seventy-eighth birthday. I overheard the doctor talking to father, "We did everything we could for your mother, but she was completely worn out. It's something that comes to all of us. The one thing that is certain in life is death."

The words jabbed me like a needle. Until then I had unrealistically imagined being on this earth for all time. I had never really contemplated death, it isn't usually done by the very young, but I knew then there had to be an end.

Father grieved silently for his mother for the bond between them had been strong. It took several years to settle the will as many of the properties she owned had sitting tenants and the market value of these in the 1950s was as low as a few hundred pounds.

Pop, without his wife's help and suffering from more frequent and severe attacks of asthma, was no longer able to continue at the Rose & Crown. Deeply saddened by his wife's death, he survived her by only two years.

The brewers, Ind Coope, quickly found new management to run the pub. It would never be the same again without Nannie's strict Victorian ways for she would never tolerate any of her customers swearing in her presence. If ever an offensive word reached her ears she would narrow her eyes in a disapproving look and was quick to remark, "What's that you said, Oxo?"

"Beg pardon, Mrs Rivers," was the customer's usual reply, for she was well respected. Some of the 'old boys', hard up for a pint, would miss Pop, for on occasions he treated them to the odd pint on the house.

The many rooms were stripped of their Victorian treasures – the heavy gilt framed oil paintings, some of highland cattle, had been sent for auction, along with china, glass, silverware and furniture, much of which was not currently fashionable and, therefore, did not raise anything like its true value. Other items simply disappeared, causing father often to wonder as to their whereabouts; among these was a Sheraton mirror that had once graced the sitting room. It had been highly admired by Nannie ever since a dealer had caught sight of it. "I'll give you a hundred pounds for that, Mrs Rivers," he had offered.

Her reply had been, "If it's worth £100 to you, it's worth £200 to me," and the mirror stayed where it was until the day she died.

The passing of his mother and step-father within a short space of time stirred father's interest in his ancestors.

He recalled that his maternal grandmother had kept a public house called the Dolphin, demolished many years ago, in Maldon High Street. His paternal grandmother lived into her nineties, frail and nearly blind, estranged from the family over an incident long ago. Her husband, a land developer, died quite young.

It was interesting to find that Nannie had five sisters, Aunts Annie, Clara, Fannie and Rose: the name of the fifth sister eluded father, for he had only been a small child when she had married. Her marriage had been resented by the family, who considered she had wed beneath her station and, for this, completely cut her off. She was never to enter the family fold again.

Three of the aunts, as well as Nannie, had lost their first husbands and remarried. Clara married Mr Gammer, later Mr Brackenborough, a Lincolnshire farmer: "Jolly, stout, with all the gold," was how father recalled him. Aunt Fanny married a wealthy Jew and ran The Hope, a busy public house that also catered for banquets and parties, in Tottenham Court Road, London. They would occasionally travel to Maldon and stay at the Blue Boar. Their coach, horses and groom would eventually arrive by road to be at their convenience when they wished to travel the district; why they never stayed at the Rose & Crown wasn't known, perhaps they felt the Blue Boar offered more luxurious accommodation. When her husband died, Fanny remarried, but her second husband turned out a real waster spending most of her money. The Hope went into decline and he disappeared, some saying he went to France, but his actual whereabouts were never established although enquiries were made.

Aunt Rose married Mr Savill and they kept the Chequers, a prominent, busy pub in Maldon. After he died she married Bill King, when they moved to the Swan Hotel, only yards away from the Chequers. Baden Savill and Basil King, as different as chalk and cheese, were her sons; during her second marriage a third child was stillborn. To manage a public house must have been in the family's blood, for Aunt Annie married Bert Sewell and kept the White Hart in Maldon; they also had two sons.

When asked about his mother's two brothers, father would say, "I was really too young to remember their names. I heard tales of the younger one. Apparently he was missing one Sunday morning. A search party was organised, but it wasn't until much later in the day they found him at Beeleigh; he had died of gunshot wounds. A verdict of accidental death was recorded."

The other brother emigrated to Australia, but returned in later life to run a piano tuning business in the Maldon district. His only form of transport was a bicycle: Australia had not made him a fortune.

I was intrigued; who was the fifth, nameless sister? Why had she been disowned by the family? I thought the way to find out might be to put an advertisement in the local newspaper asking if there were still people who knew of my father's childhood days and the Rose & Crown. I was not disappointed, for one elderly Maldonian wrote –

When I was a child our family lived in Butt Lane, at

96

that time it was known as Crown Lane. My brother, Jim, and Cyril were great friends, Cyril spent many hours in our house. They used to get up to some boyish pranks and were often found hiding in Jim Balls' empty fish barrels stacked in the yard at the back of his fish shop. My brother died many years ago. They had good clean fun and were never in trouble. I am now 85 years old, but it is good to have memories brought back.

On the strength of that letter I went to visit her, hoping she would be able to tell me more, but my hopes began to fade as I knocked at the door and saw the neglected garden, which had reverted to nature with long grass full of weeds. The house also appeared deserted, but my loud rapping attracted a neighbour who hurried across.

"Who do you want, dear?" she asked

When I mentioned the name she stiffened her bottom lip. "She won't come to the door, she has had a heart attack, you see. Afraid of the stairs, she is; lives in the top flat, you see."

Then the door opened slowly; the old lady I had come to see stood at the bottom of the stairs and must have been listening at the door, for she answered the woman, "She is nothing to do with the Council, she has come to see me."

"Oh, I see," the woman seemed surprised. "Who are you then?" she asked me.

I ignored her question and stepped inside the house as the old lady firmly closed the door behind me, leaving the neighbour fretting outside. I stood at the bottom of the stairs watching nervously while the old lady clung to the rails either side of the steep climb, every step an effort until she gained the top. "Come up now," she shouted, ""I'm afraid it takes me a long time. I haven't been out for twenty-two years, not since I had a heart attack in the Co-op store. My husband has been dead over twenty years and I've lived alone ever   since."

"Haven't you got a family?" I asked, concerned.

"Yes, two sons, but I only see them about twice a year,

nothing close about our particular family. One of my sons asked me what I wanted for my birthday; I said a card and a few kind words – I got the card and that was all."

Such apathy in a family seemed impossible to me, but, as father used to say, 'one half doesn't know how the other half lives'.

She smiled, probably at my astonishment, but she had long ago come to terms with the situation, as she had with being housebound for 22 years, over which time her inactivity had caused her to become overweight, hindering her movements, as well as causing other old age disabilities. Despite this she was cheerful and her memory was crisp as she started to relate the events of years ago.

"As I said in my letter, I knew your father well when he was a small boy, cheerful little soul he was. If Jim had been alive today he would have been able to tell you a lot more than I can. I can still hear the maid, Priscilla, calling your father in the Rose & Crown yard, 'Coom an' 'ave yar tea, hoolya, Master Cyril'. As he raced in Priscilla would often smell fish from his clothes and shout, 'If yar moother catches yer, she won't 'alf give e an iddin for gooin' in them fish barrels'."

Father had never mentioned this particular family to me, perhaps it was because he had forgotten, but more likely because the friendship had not been allowed to continue, for his mother held the belief that it was wrong to mix with those below your station.

I listened with fascination to her account of those times, knowing her family had been one of the poor of the town. For those out of work there was no money coming in to feed the large families that many produced at that time. Many felt ashamed of their status, but there was no option, hunger had driven them to live off the Parish, who provided them with meal tickets. The old lady whispered to me for fear ears outside her walls mights have heard of her family's poverty.

"I was too proud, but my sister wasn't. She would go early in the morning to the bakers, when he would sell off the stale bread and cakes for tuppence. She would bring home as many as four or five loaves and a bag of cakes, enough to last us for days.

"A good Christian woman my mother was; she saw to it that we never went hungry. Father was unemployed for long periods, for jobs in the town were few in those days. When he was able to find work his earnings were more often than not spent at the pub.

"The little money we had was usually earned by mother from taking in sewing, sometimes working through the night. She made sure we never went hungry. With six penn'orth of cods' heads she would make a tasty soup. Real wholesome meat pies she made too from three penn'orth of pieces from the butcher, two penn'orth of melts and a penn'orth of suet.

"Us kids would also go round and collect jam jars, take a bucket, sweep up the manure in the High Stret and sell that. Our reward was to buy sticks of black treacle which we sucked at for hours."

"What about Christmas?" I asked.

"We never had anything for Christmas except maybe an orange and a rabbit for Christmas dinner." The old lady paused while she reflected on her past life. "There was little opportunity in those days for the poorer classes to receive a good education. The classrooms were packed, the overspill of children took their lessons in the cloak rooms and corridors at the British School where I went to school. The building was located in front of the United Reform Church at the top of Market Hill and is still used for various functions.

"A healthy family we were, which was fortunate, for we could not have afforded a doctor. Many people died young because they could not afford to pay the doctor's bill. For the destitute, those without means and without hope, Maldon gave shelter and food in the workhouse, known as the Spike. The very mention of the name brought fear to desperately poor elderly citizens of the town. Today St Peter's hospital, as it's known, has changed little on the outside, but the inside has been modernised to care for sick, elderly patients, as well as housing units for other medical care. But for those who are still around to remember, it still bears the stigma of the workhouse."

I had been so interested, I had nearly forgotten my real reason for visiting the old lady. "Did you every know any other members of my father's family?" I asked.

"I remember your grandmother Rivers very well, she had five sisters I believe. The one I knew best was Elizabeth, we called her Liz for short, she married one of my distant relations. Her problem was drink, you know, probably had her reasons, shouldn't wonder." She was about to tell me more, but stopped, saying, "I don't like to speak ill of the dead. She had eight children, that I know. Violet, the last one I believe, died only a few months ago."

The fifth sister, Elizabeth, had been named!

FATHER THE FATALIST

We never gave up trying to persuade father to stop smoking. We knew he reaped great satisfaction and relaxation from inhaling the smoke, and after he had worked so hard it seemed wrong for us to deny him his enjoyment, but we were afraid and that drove us to try to save him from the end result of constant smoking over the years. I would watch him draw deeply on a cigarette, inhaling the smoke, and wait for him to exhale, which he rarely did. He would sit and smoke bent forward, so that the smoke curled up into his face and, over a period, turned his white forelock golden from the nicotine.

"Not another cigarette?" mother would say.

"Don't be ridiculous, Sylvia, this is the first today."

"How you can sit there and say that, I do not know."

"Because that's right, Sylvia."

"Don't bother to tell me such nonsense, Cyril."

And so it went on, mother impatient with him because he would not give it up and father not able to face the break with nicotine.

Then, suddenly, for what reason was unclear, he gave up smoking overnight in his middle sixties. He showed great willpower and determination to knife his addiction and, during the process, suffered greatly, but he never gave in, showing real force of character. His lungs stayed smoke-free for many months.

Then, on my brother's wedding day, father decided to have just one cigarette. We pleaded with him not to: after all he had been through, it just wasn't worth the risk. His reply was the usual "I know what I'm doing", but within a week he was back to smoking 20 or more a day. All his effort and suffering had been for nothing.

Mother tried to make him cut down the amount. Under her watchful eye it would seem he was smoking less. Whenever possible he would take refuge in the garage or some other quiet corner and puff away in peace. On being discovered he would try to fan away the tell-tale smoke.

"You are fooling nobody but yourself," mother would tell him.

Appearing innocent, he would say, "I really don't know what you are talking about."

One day mother came to me, saying, "Gillian, what are we going to do about your father and his attitude towards his health. He does seem to take a fatalistic approach to life. When I tell him about the dangers of smoking he just says, 'You have got to die of something'.

"Can you believe this, several years ago, when your father and I went away for a few days' holiday to Norfolk, we stayed at an old coaching inn, the only room available was at the top of a very narrow winding staircase. My first thought was, if there was a fire we should be trapped. When I mentioned this to your father he just laughed and said, 'The inn has been here for 600 years, it's not likely to burn down tonight'. At first I thought I must be dreaming when I was awakened in the early hours of the morning by the sound of fire bells. I quickly draped my dressing gown round my shoulders and rushed out of the room, calling to your father, 'Hurry, hurry, there's a fire!'

"Breathless I arrived at the bottom of the stairs, expecting to find him right behind me, but there was no sign of him. I rushed back up the stairs into the bedroom, only to find he was still lying in bed. 'What are you doing still in bed?' I shouted, 'the place is on fire, get out of bed quickly.' He turned over, saying, 'I can't smell anything'.

"Down in the cobbled courtyard the rest of the guests had assembled in their nightwear and two fire engines were in attendance. I couldn't get him out of bed, so I decided

102

I couldn't leave him, we would perish together. Five or ten minutes later, still no sign of smoke. The yard emptied, apparently it had been a false alarm. Your father turned to me and said, 'There you are, I knew there wasn't a fire, I don't know what all the fuss was about'.

"Another time there was an earthquake while we were on holiday in Yugoslavia. Everyone dashed out into the open from the hotel. I casually mentioned I hoped our money and passports would be safe. I had left them on the dressing table in the bedroom. Suddenly he vanished, after a few minutes reappearing with the money and passports. He had only been back into the hotel, taken the lift up and down and all he said was, 'I don't know why you are all worrying'."

Father would never discuss health or illnesses for he found it a depressing subject and always became aggravated when members of the family took delight in discussing their ailments. He would either walk away silently or remark, "If I went to the doctor's every time I experienced an ache or pain, I would be up there every day of my life."

If an ailment persisted, causing father pain or worry, he would eventually visit the doctor. After one occasion, having been advised by the doctor to follow a light, digestible diet, he returned home to a supper of thickly sliced fresh bread, cheese and pickles.

When plagued by a back complaint he visited a specialist. After careful examination the trouble was diagnosed and a specially made corset fitted to alleviate the pain. After nearly two hours, father, dissatisfied with the performance of the garment, freed himself from it, complaining it stabbed him in the stomach and gave him indigestion. The corset never saw light of day again, staying at the bottom of his wardrobe where he had thrown it, complaining in his usual manner about such things, "I'm not going to be humbugged up with that thing."

His back gradually improved without further attention. However, he still experienced occasional twinges of pain that he put down to age, for which there was no cure.

NOW A PROFITABLE BUSINESS

Through the public's interest in more natural foods, such as Maldon Salt, business now became very profitable. With the years of hard work and the conscientious attitude father had put into it, he now felt they were able to afford more than the necessities of life. He thought the time had now come to build the house of his choice, using the ground he owned opposite the Salt Works and selling Sylvia Villa.

He loved to give the family presents and it pleased him to give the best. I can remember being sent to the jewellers on occasions, my father saying, "You know your mother's taste; choose the best you can."

He wasn't a man to spend much on himself, but the day came when he decided to buy a boat, which wasn't surprising as he had been keen on rowing and would hire a boat sometimes of a Sunday to take us up the river. The boat was really more a gift than a buy for it seemed that a kindly old fisherman for some reason or other had given the large clinker-built rowing boat to father.

Mother was a poor swimmer and expressed her concern at the small amount of water at the bottom of the boat.

Father assured her there was nothing to worry about. "You always expect to find a little water in these old boats."

Mother, still not too sure, sat rigidly in the centre of the boat, having discarded her shoes.

Father was quite happy about it all. "Sylvia, would I take you and the children out in a boat that was likely to sink? I've told you not to worry." But the swish of the oars was no longer sending the boat gliding freely over the water.

"Cyril, we are up to our ankles in water, this boat is definitely leaking."

Father could no longer ignore this fact and suggested we might start bailing out with an old tin can that was floating in the bilge. Still showing confidence, he explained, "It's quite normal. Once the planks have swollen, it will stop taking in water."

We all started to bail out at a frantic speed, but not keeping pace with the increasing flow. Father had now turned the boat towards the shore. As we came within bottoming distance the boat sank, leaving us sitting up to our waists, safe but soaked, Clive and I enjoying the drama, with mother vowing never to go in another rowing boat.

Several years passed before boats were again mentioned. Remembering mother's vow about rowing boats father bought a clinker built cabin cruiser, christened *Red Sea*. We all looked forward to the warm, sunny, hazy days, drifting on the calm water, fishing off the nearby shores of Osea Island, anchoring off a beach, swimming, sun bathing, having picnics, getting away from it all, but more excitement was found in the anticipation.

Before any of these pleasures could be undertaken there was a great deal of work to be carried out on the boat, far more than we first thought. The vast bottom needed to be scrubbed free of its clinging barnacles. The rubbing down of the varnish seemed never-ending, for father was not happy until the job had been done properly, which some-times meant that we did more work than was needed. Father began to think that perhaps he had not done the right thing in buying a boat, especially as he suffered a bad back as a result of working too long in a cramped position.

At last, well into the boating season, she was ready to carry us on pleasure trips on the river. At first the tides arrived too early in the morning, which wasn't father's idea of enjoyment, having to rise at the crack of dawn. Then the weather was against us and, by the time that improved, the tides once again arrived too early in the day. When weather and tides were right the demands of the Salt Works interrupted our programme and it wasn't until much later in the season that we took our first trip in *Red Sea*. Instead of a full day on the river we only had about an hour and a half, for we had to return on the same tide, but a short trip was better than none at all we thought.

We bulged awkwardly in our lifejackets, except for father, who did not feel the need to wear one as he had in the past saved a friend from drowning in rough waters. We set off, father confidently steering the craft away from river-crowding sailing boats, many controlled more by the wind than by their sailors.

The engine sputtered several times, cutting in and out, not a healthy sound. The strong breeze carried the heavy vapours back into the boat, making our eyes smart and our throat irritate. Father assured us, "You always get a certain amount of that."

But we were not totally convinced, remembering the episode of the rowing boat. Mooring was a very difficult operation, for the waves created by passing motor boats bounced her away from the mooring, when the ropes missed their target she started to behave like a wild horse, with an obstinate will of her own. At last moored, father turned the key to silence the noisy engine; instead of having the desired effect, the engine roared away. The ignition had jammed, the boat lurched forward, snapping the ropes that were holding her fast. Noise and smoke engulfed the deck. Father was being taken against his will further up-river and temporarily aghast by the situation he was not able to find an immediate solution.

"Pull out your ignition leads, pull out your leads," shouted a voice from the bank. That having been done, normality returned. It took an engineer some time to sort out the problem of the crazy engine, but, after repairs had been done, *Red Sea* gave father many happy hours of cruising in the sheltered waters of the Essex coast.

Several years later *Harvest Tide* replaced *Red Sea*. The

new boat was a fine looking craft easier to maintain as she had a fibreglass hull. Our hopes ran high that she would be capable of taking us across the Channel to France. Again, anticipation was the greatest joy, for father, never a good timekeeper, missed many a tide that waited for no man, but we did have many enjoyable outings in her. Time, ever a problem, had not allowed father to use the boat as much as he would have liked and, after a lot of thought, he decided to sell her. By then the river had become more crowded with weekend sailors, many inexperienced, that made hazardous conditions for other boats on the water.

The boat was sold and, to fill the gap, mother persuaded father to buy a caravan. Once again the idea of getting away from it all was more attractive than the reality. After a few days without home comforts and with caravanning's discomforts, father decided that was not his conception of pleasure, so the caravan was sold and no more adventures for a happy retirement were engaged upon.

Father's idea of enjoyment was to be doing something and, when he was not at the Salt Works, he was working in his garden where the evidence of his green fingers was clearly visible. Although my parents had comfortable garden furniture the seats were always empty, except for visitors, who had the time to sit and rest.

Now it was quite a common occurence for the telephone to ring and someone from a magazine, daily newspaper, BBC or Pathé News (one of the first people to put Maldon Salt on the screen) would request a visit or an interview. Maldon Salt was becoming well-known, even famous. Father loved talking to the journalists, as he was, rightly, very proud of his achievements.

There is no other salt like Maldon Salt and, even with today's strict advertising rules, all the claims made for the salt cannot be disputed. It is unique, a claim few other products can venture.

One journalist after a visit to the Works was heard to say, "If Lot's wife had turned to a pillar of Maldon Salt he should have taken her with him. She would have been decorative, as well as a tasty dish."

It was easy to find captions for the articles that were written – 'Success at a pinch and straight from the seashore', 'The Curious Crystals', 'It's Crystal clear why Cyril's salt is such big business', 'Pinch of High Class Salt', were but a few. Peter Sellars, Fanny Craddock, Clement Freud, the Duke of Bedford, these and many others added their praises to the salt.

The general public were discovering how good Maldon Salt was, preferring the distinctive flavour and soft flaky crystals to that of the free flowing salt with additives.

Now they were coming to make a film about it all to be shown on television. The film crew and their equipment assembled in the yard. Father was about to join them.

"You are not going out like that," mother told him.

"What are you talking about," father was taken aback by her remark, "I'm not dressing up in a white shirt and tie, I'm going to work, not out to dinner."

"Today is different, your picture will be shown on television."

"Good God, Sylvia, I suppose you want me to wear my stiff shirt and tails."

"There is no need to be ridiculous," mother said. She quickly found a tie and slipped it under his shirt collar.

Father was still muttering, "I don't know what all this fuss and bother is about." Now more suitably dressed for the occasion, he asked mother, "How do I look now, will I pass the test?"

"You'll do," smiled mother as he walked out of the door.

The filming began. "We will have a few shots of you raking out the salt, Mr Osborne." This was the easy part, father only had to move and do as he was instructed. The words 'cut', 'retake', 'shoot', became familiar. The next part was more difficult, but not for father.

The interviewer spoke the opening sentence, "How long have you been in the salt business, Mr Osborne?"

Father was never short of words and this gave him the

opportunity to talk about his life and work, something he really enjoyed. First he told the interviewer much of the history of salt.

"Excuse me, Mr Osborne, could you stick to talking about Maldon Salt. Time is our problem, we are only allowed so many minutes. Now, will you tell exactly how Maldon Salt is made?"

The answer meant they were in for a long session, like it or not. There was no way he could shorten his description of salt making. The cameras stopped rolling, the interviewer had stopped taking notes, the whole crew were listening to father, fascinated, as they were told in full the process of making salt. The interviewer suddenly said, "As I look across the steaming salt pans I could almost visualise a crocodile emerging from the mist."

Father joined in the joke, "I can assure you it would have filtered out long before it reached the salt pans."

Then a signal brought the crew into action and the time for the interviewer's introduction. "On the banks of the River Blackwater I can feel the history of saltmaking around me for the process has changed little since salt was first made on these shores two thousand years ago.

"As we move away from the steaming pans and enter a small door on the right, the sight that meets me is quite fascinating for there are stored mountains of gleaming white salt crystals waiting to be dried, packaged, then speeded away to waiting markets, many of which are as far away as America, Australia, and Sweden, for devoted Maldon Salt customers to enjoy."

Some still shots were taken of the new blue and white one pound packets, depicting a silver salt cellar containing Maldon Salt. Filming finished and the crew thanked father for a most interesting visit. They were each given a packet of Maldon Salt, so they could test for themselves how good it was and appreciate its special flavour.

Several weeks later we were told of the day and time the Salt Works would be shown on television. Before the programme began we seated ourselves comfortably for what we thought was a full-length feature. The familiar face of the interviewer came on the screen. "Today I am in the historic town of Maldon in Essex, where the Maldon Salt Company stands on the banks of the River Blackwater," he announced, then went on to give a brief description of the history of salt-making.

Father appeared next, giving a considerably shortened explanation of how the gleaming salt crystals were made. After a fleeting shot of the new packet, the programme ended abruptly. It had barely lasted four minutes.

"Well, I'm damned, after all that," was all father managed to say.

Local people who had seen the programme would stop father and say jokingly, "How's the film star then?"

Father's next appearance in the public eye was when Brian Johnston introduced him on the radio in *Down Your Way*. The preparation before the recording was finally edited had been done in the relaxed atmosphere of the home. Father, the good conversationalist he always was, talked freely when asked questions, the recording tapes covering more than his allocated time. At this point Brian Johnston seemed somewhat concerned; interrupting the tape, he consulted the editor, "We have already done six minutes and we haven't finished the process yet."

"Don't worry, it's excellent, I'm quite happy, I assure you."

With this reassurance Mr Johnston continued his questions, "You showed us piles of salt that looked like pure white snow drifts. Do you colour it in any way?"

"No," father answered, "there are no chemicals or additives used in the manufacture of our product from start to finish."

"What about the taste, is it different from other salts?"

"Oh, yes. Immediately you can tell the difference, the salt crystals have a soft mellow taste, as opposed, shall we say, to being hard and attacking, the word I believe, is non-deliquescent."

The questions were numerous, ending with "Are you the

only people who are producing this crystal sea salt?"

Father proudly answered, "We are the only people who are producing these particular salt crystals in the world today."

"Well done, long may you continue to produce it."

To end the programme father was asked for his choice of music and he had no hesitation in selecting 'Strangers on the Shore' by Acker Bilk, being associated with the sea, as it seemed an appropriate choice.

"Well done, very good, that was excellent," said the editor.

Brian Johnston again expressed concern, "I honestly think it's too long, I don't see how you are going to cut it."

"I'll cut it, don't worry. I'm delighted with it."

True to his word, the history of Maldon Salt was condensed into a very enjoyable programme.

PUNCH,

OR THE LONDON

CHARIVARI.

October 10. 1874.]

" MAKING THE BEST OF IT."

First Artisan. "Been to the Sea-side this Year, Bill!"
Second Artisan. "No; it don't run to it, My Boy. A Pint of S'rimps and 'alf a pound o' Tidman's Sea-salt 'll be about my form!"

CHANGES IN THE PIPE LINE

Father was not ambitious to enlarge the Salt Works to any degree. He now had as much business as he could handle himself and was not prepared to take chances on expansion, although it seemed the trade was there. Father had all he wanted now, achieved through his years of hard work, and that was as far as he felt he could go.

The final worry he inflicted on himself was to have a new packaging room built. Before that two or three conscientious ladies were employed on a temporary basis to package the salt, depending on the orders, working in a small annex where a coal fire burnt continuously, winter and summer, not for their benefit, for sometimes the heat was too great, but to maintain the right atmosphere needed to dry the salt. On hot summer days the ladies worked and wilted uncomplainingly. To reduce the temperature when it was too high even for the good of the salt, cold water was hosed over the corrugated roof, giving the workers a little respite from the heat.

The new extension brought design, planning and building problems above average to contend with, causing father a great deal of worry. He was now at an age when most men retire and, although he never completely finished work, for to do that would mean for him retiring from life, he handed over the actual running of the business to my brother, Clive. It had always been assumed that he would take up the reins and this was the appropriate time.

Clive could see that changes were needed to bring the Works into line with modern methods. Although father had not wanted to make such changes himself he rarely queried anything Clive did, having total confidence in his son.

Tom Brown could see the changes about to be made and was reluctant to accept them and he decided, therefore, to leave. It was with sadness that we saw him go for he had been an honest and hardworking employee for many years, a popular character well versed in the happenings of the local community. An era had now passed, for other employees about to be engaged, would never experience the hard work involved in salt making.

Until this time mother had managed the accounts and business work at home, as there was no office on the site. This was soon to be changed when planning permission for an office was sought.

Then there were the furnaces, which were then very much out of date. They were converted to automatic coal feed, doing away with the clinkering out of the old system. Although this was an improvement, it was still far from ideal. Clive had an even better idea and was soon discussing the possibilities of the furnaces being fired by natural gas, which would mean a much cleaner operation and less work for the employees. At this father had some reservation. All his life he had known exactly how the salt would turn out. Would they be taking too big a chance and alter the famous crystals – perhaps not even make salt at all?

Clive could see no reason why gas would not work, although he admitted there was an element of doubt in everything. To eliminate this doubt as far as possible he conducted a great deal of research. He contacted Eastern Gas Technical Services, hoping to smooth out the problems through their expertise. It was the first time they had been asked to participate in work of this kind and they became interested in the challenge that arose, setting to work on one furnace for a trial conversion. The industrial staff at South Anglia designed and engineered the gas burner equipment, then installed it ready for the changeover.

The design incorporated special interlinked damper systems to reduce heat loss via the flue when the burner was not firing, which contributed greatly to saving fuel. Modifications to further improve the efficiency of the operation were carried out by Eastern Gas. The gas channels in the brickwork underneath the pans were re-designed, which increased the rate of heat transfer to the brine as well as evenly distributing the temperatures beneath the pan, enabling a larger quantity of sea water to be evaporated in a given time.

The automatic coal feed system was left in place, a precaution should the gas heating not prove satisfactory, but the trials proved successful and the second furnace was converted. The outcome of this was that the Maldon Crystal Salt Company won the Gas Energy Management Award in 1981 for their contribution towards energy conservation. A 26% saving on fuel was achieved due to the efficiency of the new heating system installed.

An added bonus that had not been expected from the conversion to gas was that there were far fewer 'blow ups'. Under the old system concentrated heat often played on one particular area of the pan, causing the limescale already formed on the bottom – like fur in a kettle – to explode. The tiny fragments of scale then had to be picked from the salt, a laborious and time-consuming task. Very often, before this was allowed to happen, the pans were 'chipped'. Once every three weeks or so father would hammer away at the scale in the pans, breaking it loose from the bottoms. This operation could take up to a full day before the pans were scale free, washed out and ready to use. It then took a few more days before they were back in full production, as the first few makings of salt were generally of a low yield, until the pans had been 'pickled' with salt water.

The packers were now finding it hard to cope with increasing orders, for packing by hand was slow and it was clear that the packaging system must be updated. It was found that there was no machine available that completely suited our requirements, simply because the market had not been asked to cater for a product such as ours.

114

Clive had no technical training in that field, but he conceived ideas that could be put into practice and, in consultation with the manufacturers, made modifications to existing equipment. On the drawing board he designed a new packaging area, ready for the installation of the new machines. 'From the past into the future' ran the caption in the local 'papers and various magazines.

Maldon's oldest industry has taken a great leap forward with the help of 20th century technology. For centuries the famous crystal salt has been packed by hand before being shipped off to Harrods, Sainsbury's, Fortnum & Mason, not to mention a thriving export trade with Sweden. Now a brand new packaging machine has trebled the Company's output without increasing the number of staff.

Clive was already planning to build another area on to the packaging room to be used as extra storage space.

The reservoir that trapped the salt water from the river was the next for alteration. It was filled in and replaced by huge plastic holding tanks.

The demand for the salt still increased, so a third pan was installed for increasing daily production by around a further 7 hundredweight.

By this time the Maldon Crystal Salt Company was also the proprietor of Tidman's Sea Salt, a well-known and long-established company involved in the importation and marketing of natural table and bath sea salts. As long ago as 1874 a cartoon in *Punch* referred to Tidman's Sea Salt.

Gone forever were the days of coal carting or standing on the riverbank in the early hours of a freezing morning waiting for the high tides. Bagging up the salt in hessian bags, re-arranging them around the hot brickwork of the pans in an effort to dry the salt, and the weekly washing of the bags would never be necessary again, for a special formulated gas oven dried the salt in plastic trays.

The only backbreaking job now was the loading and unloading of lorries, often manhandling many tons at a time. Even this was on the way out as a forklift truck was bought, taking away the lifting and saving many hours.

Although buttons, switches and timeclocks operated the furnaces, expertise was still needed to calculate the reduction or increase in temperatures, so vital in the making of Maldon Salt. But it has to be admitted that work was far easier and cleaner.

Father would watch the forklift truck slide its forks under a pallet that held a tonne of salt, trundle away and effortlessly stack it within minutes. "Bloody marvellous," he would say, shaking his head. "I wish I'd had one of those in my day, instead of shifting twenty tons of salt by hand."

Father always experienced slight irritation when he saw the 'lads' having their break in the canteen. There they would be with their feet up, listening to the radio, reading the newspaper and munching sandwiches in a comfortable warm atmosphere. His mind would go back and recall the hardships he had experienced. How he had worked without stopping and resting, let alone reading or listening to the radio. He has arrived in the office many times, saying, "In my day you were lucky if you had any break at all." But times had changed, especially for the worker, and, in the main, Father took it all in his stride. Naturally he would compare these times with the old days and would always be ready to chat with anyone about bygone times.

As time went on, Philip came to work for us, to ease Clive of some of the increasing workload in production and leave him free to concentrate on business within the office.

We had persuaded mother and father to take a much-needed holiday. This was not easy in father's case as he always found reasons for staying at home, anticipating the possible problems that could arise at the Works; it had always been the same and it wasn't going to change now.

"Just go and don't worry, everything will be O.K." Clive assured father. Mother, determined that they should have a break, went ahead and made the holiday arrangements.

Under normal circumstances Clive, now being familiar with the running of the business, would certainly have experienced no problems, but for the following two weeks he would not be at the Works as he had been called to the Caribbean on a government fact-finding mission to report on the possibility of reviving the once-thriving salt industry in the Turks and Caicos Islands. A more convenient time for the trip would have been helpful, but the airline tickets and arrangements had all been finalised.

Father had been instructing me for days on all eventualities that could occur and how to deal with them. He was still talking as he backed the car up the drive, "You'll be alright then. Oh, and Gillian, don't forget to –"

Mother cut him short, "Come along, Cyril, you have told her everything."

He wound up the window reluctantly; I could see he still wanted to make absolutely sure I had understood everything he had earlier told me, but mother was stressing they would be late unless they left at once. I waved until the car was out of sight. There was no calling them back, as they would soon be on a 'plane for Portugal.

At first everything ran smoothly with no production problems. What could go wrong? I asked myself as I dealt confidently with the office work, believing father would be pleased on his return from holiday. As promised, I checked the pans late each night, long after the workers had gone home, confident about it all. One Friday night, while carrying out my late duty, I noticed there was more steam than usual rising from one of the pans, but didn't attach much importance to this, for the salt was making well. I checked at the stokehold where the furnaces roared, cutting in and out as programmed, remembering the words of the workmen before leaving, "Everything has been set, there is nothing to worry about."

Remembering those words I dismissed any thoughts that an error could have been made. On Saturday no one worked, so I made it my job to go and check the Works that morning. I knew immediately I entered by the side door that all was not well, the atmosphere was damp and clammy, condensation dripping noisily from the overhead beams on to the concrete floor. As I arrived at the first pan my apprehension turned to horror. Something had gone terribly wrong! The boiling process had continued all night, every drop of water had evaporated, the furnaces having failed to cut out, the dial being set incorrectly. The excessive heat on the dry metal of the pan had caused it to buckle and the salt had been burnt into solid mounds welded to the metal in places.

I was rooted to the spot as I took in the awful sight. Thousands of pounds of damage must have been done. I was alone with this shocking situation. I switched off the furnace, too late. Momentarily there seemed to be no one to turn to, then I thought of Sue, Clive's wife. If it was possible to sort something out, I knew she would be the one most likely to find an answer. She came to share the problem with me.

Before we were able to estimate how much damage had been done, it was necessary to remove the mounds of burnt salt from the pan. It wasn't simply a question of shovelling it away, first we had to use an axe to chip away at the salt bonded to the metal. Dressed in waterproof gear, helmet and goggles for protection, Sue and I worked all day until all the salt was cleared.

It was then time to call in the welder who had previously serviced the pans. On first inspection he thought a panel could be satisfactorily welded on to repair the worst of the damage, saving the large expense of a new pan. This was done and we were able to put the pan into production again.

We swore the welder to secrecy over this, for if father ever got to hear he would never take another holiday or, in fact, ever leave the Works again. When Clive returned home, his main concern was that father should not know, for he wanted to save him any worry – and save us from endless lectures!

After reprimanding the workmen for their gross error, Clive immediately had an alarm system installed whereby it would never be possible again for the pans to continue boiling uninterrupted.

Clive Osborne in the stokehold, now transformed by modern technology. Compare this with the cover photograph of the same location

119

THE FINAL EPISODE

Life at the Salt Works continued much in the same vein, with Clive putting in long hours, planning and improving wherever possible. Trade escalated with his expertise in knowing how to create demand. The result was increased business coming our way, such as a large export order to Sweden, reported in one newspaper –

Family firm that's worth its salt

A small Maldon family firm has won a large export order from Sweden which they hope will be the shape of things to come. The order was for 2,200 cases of locally produced salt which filled a complete container for shipment to Gotenberg, Sweden. The order was packed in the standard Maldon Sea Salt packets, specially printed in Swedish. Mr Clive Osborne, Managing Director of the Maldon Crystal Salt Company, said about 25% of production accounted for export with the rest for the home market. Other places the firm exports to include Australia, America, Norway, Singapore, but this is the largest order yet, and the firm hope it will lead to more.

The hope came true, for the Swedes, being health conscious, appreciated our natural salt with no additives and repeated their orders.

The silent praises were for father, who through the years had struggled on during difficult times to hand over a valuable business to his children. Father, seeing the way business was shaping, happily shed most of his worries, but continued to spend many hours at the Works, keeping an eye on things and generally doing what needed attention.

He would spend as long as it took, for all work had to be done thoroughly.

Father would always make do and patch up as he had been forced in the past and he wasn't going to change now. However, he never argued or tried to stop Clive when he wanted to go ahead with what seemed to father a very costly expansion programme for he knew Clive would never undertake anything without researching it first, usually making the end result fruitful.

"I must say, I never could spend vast sums of money easily, it was never in me to take too much of a gamble," I heard father telling Clive.

"Well, father," explained Clive, "you have to spend money to make money."

Father agreed, but he was pleased to leave this kind of decision to Clive.

The photograph hanging on the office wall prompted father to comment, "It makes me think of the old days, seeing that old photograph hanging there. That was the time the old Salt Works lorry had been dressed up for the Maldon carnival. You can see poor old Arthur Thorogood sitting in a pile of salt in the middle of the lorry." He then pointed to the photograph, "There is Vic Dorrington in the front and John Brown in the back. When I took over the business I had a model T Ford 30 cwt lorry, considered to be quite something in those days; it had a running board to stand on. Unfortunately I didn't have it too long as it rusted and started to deteriorate."

Clive subtly indicated he wanted to get on with some work by placing his hand on the telephone in readiness to making a call, but father carried on talking oblivious. Not wishing to interrupt father's enjoyment of the past Clive relaxed into his chair and listened.

"The next lorry I bought was in 1937. ENO 34, she lasted me about 15 years, mind you, only because I looked after her, she would probably have gone on even longer had she not been involved in a smash up. A sand and ballast lorry carrying 10 tons of ballast suddenly applied his brakes to avoid colliding with an Eastern National bus. Although I braked immediately it didn't prevent me from crashing into the lorry in front. The 5 tons of salt I was carrying at the time shot up against the cab, crushing it, preventing my escape. I was eventually rescued by being pulled through the window. The lorry was the only casualty with a bent chassis weakened by years of wear and tear.

"I remember the time I was without a lorry and borrowed an old army jeep from Jimmy Gozzett. I ignored the weight stipulation and overloaded the jeep with the result the wheels fell off. I can laugh about it now, but it wasn't funny at the time, I can tell you. Oh, well, I'll let you people get on with your work," and he would walk out of the office. Such chats would have been commonplace had the office not been busy.

As time went on there was a noticeable deterioration in father's health; years of continuous smoking and hard work were now clearly visible. Still he worked on uncomplaining, rarely commenting on his ill health. Only for the last few months of his life was he unable to visit the Salt Works, his lifeline.

As he sat at home, pensive, out of character, I knew his thoughts were not for sharing; it was now a time for quietly reminiscing, a time of sadness, but a time to reflect and feel thankful for what life had offered. His early years at the Rose & Crown had been a happy record of pleasurable memories. His sense of humour lightened the darker moments of life, if not for himself, for others.

Today what would have meant hardship for many, working without the implements of modernity, father had contentedly accepted, for it was the only way in those times to run a business and survive. There were always those who would say to him, "You're lucky to have your own business."

Father would agree with that, but when they said, "So as you can take time off whenever you like," father would laugh and say, "Believe me, you don't know what it's all about. If I get a week's holiday, I consider myself to be lucky. As for taking days here and there, who do you think is going to run my business when I'm away?"

When speaking to mother on the subject, he would say, "They don't think either about all the worries attached to running your own business. Sometimes I think it would be nice to have a job from nine to five and no worries."

Mother, amused at his remarks, would say, "You know that would never have suited you."

He enjoyed his days as a salt maker, reaping satisfaction from his efforts. The importance of time was becoming more of a major factor in the 60s when business increased considerably. Father, never a clockwatcher, would not be put under pressure by watching the clock, for he would always find time to chat with customers, usually about changing times and remembering the past. His day of work was never planned to finish at a given time, he would finish when he had completed his planned jobs and not before. It was the way he preferred to do things.

He would often say with pride, "My family have never given me any trouble and there is not too many that can say that truthfully."

He had no regrets, except in his seventy-seventh year he did say, "Never let the grandchildren smoke."

Now there was only the past and the present, he had never been one to talk of the future, knowing its uncertainty. As time went on willpower and determination were not sufficient to restore his health. Encouragingly I told him, "You will get better," believing this to be true.

"We hope so," he answered, out of character. Tears immediately clouded my vision at the realisation of the meaning of his words, for in the past he had never had the slightest doubt that he would overcome all ailments.

On 26th March, 1985, the Union Jack flew at half mast, the Salt Works were silent, the furnaces switched off and the packing room empty, no salt would be made that day. These were the marks of respect for my Father whose life had ended that day and whose involvement in the works had lasted most of his seventy-seven years...